Lecture Notes in Computer Science

T0238399

Commenced Publication in 1973
Founding and Former Series Editors:
Gerhard Goos, Juris Hartmanis, and Jan van Leeuwen

Abdelkader Hameurlain (Ed.)

Data Management in Grid and Peer-to-Peer Systems

First International Conference, Globe 2008
Turin, Italy, September 3, 2008
Proceedings

 Springer

Volume Editor

Abdelkader Hameurlain
Paul Sabatier University
Institut de Recherche en Informatique de Toulouse (IRIT)
118, route de Narbonne, 31062 Toulouse Cedex, France
E-mail: hameur@irit.fr

Library of Congress Control Number: Applied for

CR Subject Classification (1998): D.2, C.2.4, D.1.3, H.2.4, E.1

LNCS Sublibrary: SL 3 – Information Systems and Application, incl. Internet/Web
and HCI

ISSN   0302-9743
ISBN-10   3-540-85175-5 Springer Berlin Heidelberg New York
ISBN-13   978-3-540-85175-2 Springer Berlin Heidelberg New York

Springer is a part of Springer Science+Business Media

springer.com

© Springer-Verlag Berlin Heidelberg 2008
Printed in Germany

Typesetting: Camera-ready by author, data conversion by Scientific Publishing Services, Chennai, India
Printed on acid-free paper   SPIN: 12453375   06/3180   5 4 3 2 1 0

Preface

First International Conference on Data Management in Grid and Peer-to-Peer (P2P) Systems, Globe 2008

Data management can be achieved by different types of systems: from centralized file management systems to grid and P2P systems passing through distributed systems, parallel systems, and data integration systems. An increase in the demand of data sharing from different sources accessible through networks has led to proposals for virtual data integration approach. The aim of data integration systems, based on the mediator-wrapper architecture, is to provide uniform access to multiple distributed, autonomous and heterogeneous data sources. Heterogeneity may occur at various levels (e.g., different hardware platforms, operating systems, DBMS).

For more than ten years, research topics such as grid and P2P systems have been very active and their synergy has been pointed out. They are important for scale distributed systems and applications that require effective management of voluminous, distributed, and heterogeneous data. This importance comes out of characteristics offered by these systems (e.g., autonomy and the dynamicity of nodes, decentralized control for scaling). Today, the grid and P2P systems intended initially for intensive computing and file sharing are open to the management of voluminous, heterogeneous, and distributed data in a large-scale environment. The management of large distributed and heterogeneous data in grid and P2P systems raises new problems, which present real challenges, mainly: (a) resource discovery and allocation (selection), (b) distributed query processing and optimization, (c) task placement, (d) monitoring services for query optimization, (e) replication and caching, (f) cost models, (g) autonomic data management, and (h) security aspects.

The main objective of the First International Conference on Data Management in Grid and P2P Systems was to present the latest results in research and applications, to identify new issues, and to shape future directions.

In response to the call for papers, 23 papers were submitted from around the world. Of these, 10 papers were accepted for publication in the proceedings. The selected papers related to grid and P2P systems are mainly focused on P2P storage systems, cache management, P2P data integration systems and querying grid and P2P systems.

I would like to express thanks to the authors who submitted papers and to the Program Committee for the thorough review process. Special thanks go to Roland Wagner, A Min Tjoa, Gabriela Wagner (FAW, University of Linz), and the local organizers.

June 2008   Abdelkader Hameurlain

Organization

Program Chair

Abdelkader Hameurlain   IRIT, Paul Sabatier University, Toulouse, France

Program Committee

Maha Abdallah	LIP6 Laboratory, Paris VI, Paris 6 University, France
Frederic Andres	University of Advanced Studies, Tokyo, Japan
Djamal Benslimane	LIRIS, University of Lyon 1, France
Peter Brezany	University of Vienna, Austria
Lionel Brunie	LIRIS, INSA de Lyon, France
Claude Chrisment	IRIT, Paul Sabatier University, Toulouse, France
Michel Daydé	IRIT, INPT - ENSEEIHT, Toulouse, France
Bruno Defude	INT, Evry, France
Shahram Ghandeharizadeh	University of Southern California, USA
Tasos Gounaris	University of Manchester, UK
Anirban Mondal	University of Tokyo, Japan
Franck Morvan	IRIT, Paul Sabatier University, Toulouse, France
Kjetil Nørvåg	Norwegian University of Science and Technology,Trondheim, Norway
Salvatore Orlando	University of Venice, Italy
Florence Sedes	IRIT, Paul Sabatier University, Toulouse, France
Mário J. Silva	University of Lisbon, Portugal
Heinz Stockinger	Swiss Institute of Bioinformatics, Lausanne, Switzerland
David Taniar	Monash University, Australia
A. Min Tjoa	IFS, Vienna University of Technology, Austria
Genoveva Vargas-Solar	LIG, Grenoble University, France
Roland Wagner	FAW, University of Linz, Austria
Alexander Wöhrer	IFS, Vienna University of Technology, Austria
Wolfram Wöß	Institute for Scientific Computing, University of Vienna, Austria

External Reviewers

Riad Mokadem
Pilar Villamil

Table of Contents

A File Transfer Service with Client/Server, P2P and Wide Area Storage Protocols

Gilles Fedak, Haiwu He, and Franck Cappello

INRIA Saclay, Grand-Large, Orsay, F-91893
LRI, Univ Paris-Sud, CNRS, Orsay, F-91405
`fedak@lri.fr`

Abstract. The last years have seen the emergence of new P2P file distribution protocols such as BitTorrent as well as new Wide Area Storage based on Web Service technology. In this paper, we propose a multi-protocol file transfer service which supports client/server and P2P protocols, as well as Wide Area Storage such as Amazon S3. We describe the mechanisms used to ensure file transfer monitoring and reliability. We explain how to plug-in new or existing protocols and we give evidence of the versatility of the framework by implementing the HTTP, FTP and BitTorrent protocols and access to the Amazon S3 and IBP Wide Area Storage. Finally, we report on basic performance evaluation of our framework, both in a Grid context and on the Internet.

Keywords: P2P, CDN, Wide Area Storage, File transfer.

1 Introduction

The last years have seen the emergence of new distributed protocols which enable large scale content management and distribution. Researchers of DHT's (Distributed Hash Tables) [SMK+01, MM02, RD01] and collaborative content distribution network such as BitTorrent [Coh03] or Avalanche [GR05, FM06], and Wide Area Storage (WAS) such as IBP [BBF+02] or Oceanstore[Ka00] offer various tools that could be of interest to build next generation of data management services or application. As a movement of balance, the focus have more recently shifted towards a new class of services called Web Services, which are architectured as a classical client/server protocol based on web technologies. One of the key feature of Web Services is the ability to compose them through a set of technologies based on various flavors of XML-RPC such as SOAP or REST. As example of these new services, Amazon S3 [aws, ama] proposes an on-line, low-cost, highly available data storage service with a simple on-demand billing model[1].

However, to utilize these tools effectively, one needs to bring together these components into a comprehensive framework. The BitDew environment that we have presented in a previous publication [FHC08] suits this purpose by providing an environment for data management and distribution for large scale distributed application. The objective of this paper is to describe the key component responsible for data transfer, namely the Data Transfer Service and the Transfer Manager API.

---

[1] S3 Service is for storage (currently at a rate of $0.15/GB/Month), data transfers (at 0.10/GB of data transfered) and data requests ($0.01/1000PUT or GET).

A. Hameurlain (Ed.): Globe 2008, LNCS 5187, pp. 1–11, 2008.

This service features multi-protocols data transfer, highly asynchronous transfer, reliability, performance monitoring and graphical interface. In this paper, we describe the architecture of the service, the mechanism to control out-of-band file transfer and how to integrate new or existing protocols. We give evidence that our service is able to cope with classical client/server protocol such as HTTP and FTP, with P2P or collaborative content delivery protocol such as BitTorrent, with Wide Area Storage such as IBP or Amazon S3. Overall, this service can be used in any application needing multi-protocol file transfer library. BitDew's data transfer service will provide the application with concurrent, reliable and P2P transfers. It is also a mean of leveraging future enhancements of P2P or WAS protocols without modifying the existing applications. In this paper, we also report on new performance evaluation both in a controlled Grid environment and in the Internet context.

The rest of the paper is organized as follows. In Section 2, we give the background of our researches, in Section 3, we give an overview of BitDew and its architecture, in Section 4, we describe the principles, programming interface and implementation of the File Transfer Service, and we report on performance evaluation in Section 5. Finally we present related work in Section 6 and we conclude the paper in Section 7.

2   Background

The first category of file transfer protocol is the classical client/server protocol such as FTP or HTTP. Because these protocols are standardized, there exists many implementation of the server and the client. Client/server file transfer protocols are usually synchronous, in the sense that the client and the server operates simultaneously during the whole file transfer, and the beginning and the end of a file transfer is detected at the same time on the sender and the receiver of a file. For developers, the client protocol is often provided as a library whose function calls to file transfer are blocking. As a consequence it is easy to detect the end of a file transfer. Furthermore protocols usually report error code to signal its user that a file transfer was not authorized or has failed.

The second category of file transfer protocol is Collaborative Content Distribution (CCD) protocol, often featured as *parallel download* in P2P applications. The key idea is to divide the file in a list of chunks. Immediately after a peer downloads a chunk from another peer, the peer serves the block for the other peers in the network, thus behaving itself as a server. A good example of CCD or P2P protocol is the BitTorrent protocol.

BitTorrent is a popular file distribution system which aims at avoiding the bottleneck of FTP servers when delivering large and highly popular files. A peer will first get all the informations about the file to download in a special static file called a .torrent. A .torrent file contains the SHA1 signature for all the chunks composing the file and the location of a central agent called the *tracker*, which helps the peers to connect each other. In a BitTorrent network, trackers are responsible for keeping a list of informations about the peers: IP address, port to contact, file downloads. When a peer requests a file, it first asks the tracker a list of contact informations about the peers who are downloading the same file. The tracker does not organize transfers of the chunks between the peers; all data movements are decided locally by a peer according to local informations collected on its neighbors. From this list of peers, the downloader asks its neighbors for the transfer of the file chunks. Peers select autonomously to which host to send chunks based on the following rules : 1) no more than 4 file uploads are running at a time, 2) selection of the upload peer is based on the best transfer rates averaged on the last 20-second time frame and 3) once every 30 seconds, a random selection of a fifth peers to upload is performed which helps to discover peer with a better bandwidth. Because several peers collaborate to the transfer of a single file, it is impossible to monitor the file transfer from the sender-side only, as it is common with client/server protocol. Thus the ending of the file transfer as well as file-integrity check must be performed on the receiver-side.

The emergence of Web2.0 service offers new opportunity for large remote file storage. Amazon's Simple Storage (S3) is a set of Web Service ruled by the Amazon Web Service (AWS) company. Tens of thousands of computer system around the world support Amazon S3 service to provide a scalable data storage system that aims to offer very high availability, low data-access latency, and long data durability [aws]. From March 2006, more and more home users and all kind of business enterprises started to benefit this services. A record of overs 800 million data objects stored has been reported [ama].

Once registered with a valid credit card, users are given access keys which allow to use the service through a SOAP or REST messaging protocol. To manage data with the S3's API, users create *buckets*, which are slot created in the whole S3's storage and which contains one or more *objects*. *Buckets* are like folders or containers. They have a unique name in S3 global namespace. Users can use them to organize their data. An access control policy is applied to each *bucket*. The audit report is also generated for each *bucket* to charge the users every month. *Objects* are any sequence of bytes whose size is between 1 and 5GB. Users can upload and download data using HTTP, then data can be shared using the BitTorrent protocol.

Logistical Networking [BBF+02] is a technology for sharing network storage, which provides an easy scaling. IBP (Internet Backplane Protocol) is a middleware to use and manage remote storage by allocation of "byte arrays". "exNode" as an inode for network distributed files is developed to access stored data. L-Bone (Logistical Backbone), a group of facilities can provide application-independent, free location, high-performance access to storage of network.

3   Overview of BitDew

In this section we give a brief overview of the BitDew runtime environment in order to understand how our file transfer service is built. We orient readers towards this publication [FHC08] for further details.

3.1   BitDew Principles and Architecture

BitDew is a programmable environment for automatic and transparent data management and distribution. It is originally designed for Desktop Grid but it can be easily integrated in any distributed application requiring high features file transfer.

BitDew relies on a programming model that provides developers with an abstraction for complex tasks associated with large scale data management, such as life cycle, transfer, placement, replication and fault tolerance. While maintaining a high level of

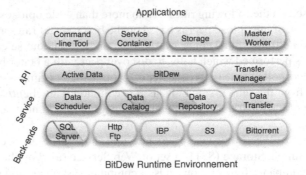

Fig. 1. The BitDew software architecture. The upper part of the figure shows distributed applications designed using BitDew. Lower parts are the three layers composing the BitDew run-time environment : the API layer, the service layer and the back-ends layer. Colors illustrate how various components of different layers combine together. For instance, the Transfer Manager API uses two services : Data Repository and Data Transfer, which in turn use five back-ends : SQL Server, HTTP/FTP , IBP, S3 and BitTorrent protocol.

transparency, users still have the possibility to enhance and fine tune this platform by interacting directly with the runtime environment.

BitDew relies on 5 metadata which drives the runtime environment : *i*) *replication* indicates how many occurrences of data should be available at the same time in the system, *ii*) *fault tolerance* controls the resilience of data in presence of machine crash, *iii*) *lifetime* is a duration, absolute or relative to the existence of other data, which indicates when a datum is obsolete, *iv*) *affinity* drives movement of data according to dependency rules, *v*) *transfer protocol* gives the runtime environment hints about the file transfer protocol appropriate to distribute the data. Programmers tag each data with these simple attributes, and simply let the BitDew runtime environment manage operations of data creation, deletion, movement, replication, as well as fault tolerance.

Figure 1 illustrates the layered BitDew software architecture upon which distributed application can be developed. The architecture is divided in three layers. The uppermost layers, the API layer, which offers various programming interface to the environment. In this paper, we will describe in depth the Transfer Manager API which offers a nonblocking interface to concurrent file transfers, allowing users to probe for transfer, to wait for transfer completion, to create barriers and to tune the level of transfers concurrency.

The intermediate level is the service layer which implements the API : data storage and transfers, replicas and volatility management. In our system model, nodes are divided in 2 categories : server nodes and client nodes. Server nodes run various independent services which compose the runtime environment: Data Repository (DR), Data Catalog (DC), Data Transfer (DT) and Data Scheduler (DS).

The fault model we consider for node running the DT service is the transient fault where a host is assumed to be restarted by administrators after a failure. Thus, we save every information in a stable memory, an SQL database, to allow restart of the DT server in a coherent state. The BitDew protocol is connectionless, where all communication are initiated by the client nodes to the DT server. This facilitates the deployment, because only the DT service node needs to be reachable from the outside world. Failure of client nodes is detected by the mean of timeout on periodical heartbeats.

File transfers are performed by running simultaneously two protocols side by side : the BitDew protocol, which is in charge of controlling the file transfer, and the *out-of-band* protocol which performs the actual file transfer.

In this paper we describe the file transfer service which corresponds to a subset of the BitDew architecture, namely the Transfer Manager API, the Data Transfer Service (DT), the Data Repository Service (DR) and the implementation of several out-of-band file transfer back-ends : HTTP/FTP, S3, IBP and BitTorrent. In comparison with our previous publication [FHC08], we give detailed information about the management of file transfers, we describe new protocols back-ends (S3 and IBP) and we give unpublished performance evaluation.

4 Presentation of the File Transfer Service

In this section, we detail the features and the various components of the file transfer service.

4.1 Programming Interface

The file transfer service allows users to launch concurrent file transfers and select a file transfer protocol amongst the various out-of-band protocols supported. Whatever the file transfer protocol selected, transfers are all handled the same way : transfers are concurrent, reliable and methods to launch transfers are always non-blocking.

We now give an overview of the different steps to achieve a file transfer. First, it is necessary to configure the BitDew runtime environment, of which file transfer service is a part. A key element of the environment is the Data Repository service, which provides both file storage and remote file access. For instance, configuring a DR accessible through a FTP server consists of setting up the file server IP address or host name and port. Configuring the BitTorrent protocol consists of providing the tracker address and a base URL to download/upload the torrents. The BitDew runtime allows to mix several DR services enabling complex architecture where data can be stored in multiple sources.

After initialization, users can perform file transfer. The easiest solution is to take advantage of the TupleSpace-like functions provided by the BitDew API. Following this approach, users create slots in the data space and simply perform push and get operations of file into this slot. In this case, BitDew will automate most of the file transfer operation. The second approach allows developers to control more precisely the file transfer. Users first create Protocol (objects representing the protocol and allowing security configuration of the protocol, such as password/login for FTP user) and Locators (objects representing remote and local file references) and the file transfer services will create and manage transfers according to these definitions. It is noteworthy that the TransferManager API offers non-blocking functions to the programmer even if the protocol is synchronous and the protocol library functions are blocking.

Finally, each out-of band transfer is queued and managed concurrently. The API offers function to probe for transfers state, namely to probe if the transfer is complete, waiting, stalled or on-going. Several functions allows to create barriers, either by blocking until a specific set of transfers complete or by waiting for all remaining transfers to finish.

4.2 Integrating Out-of-Band File Transfer Protocols

Figure 2 presents the framework to integrate existing or new client/server, P2P or WAS file transfer protocols. Each out-of-band protocol is represented as an OOBTransfer object within the internal transfer management engine. thus to plug-in a new file transfer protocol, a programmer has to implement the OOBTransfer interface. This interface can be implemented in two flavors, depending on whether the methods launching and controlling the actual file transfer are blocking or not. Programmer chooses the blocking (resp. non blocking) interface if the protocol functions are blocking (resp. non blocking).

For instance, the declaration of the FtpTransfer class, using the blocking library provided by the Apache commons-net package would be:

```
public class FtpTransfer extends OOBTransferImpl
        implements BlockingOOBTransfer , OOBTransfer throws OOBTransferException;
```

Most of the synchronous C/S and WAS protocols are provided as library with blocking communications. However, the situation is more complex with P2P protocol, which features non-blocking communication, whose implementations are provided as libraries or as daemons. Note, that the former is very popular for P2P protocol embedded in file sharing application. A daemon runs forever in the background and a GUI issues users

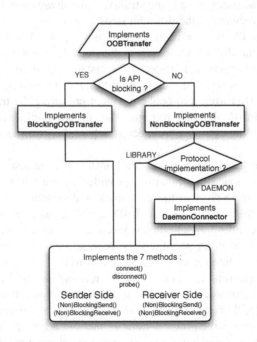

Fig. 2. Flowchart to implement out-of-band transfer

Table 1. Out-of-Bad File Transfer Implementation. C/S stands for Client/Server and WAS for Wide Area Storage.

Protocol		Name	Interface	Implementation
HTTP	C/S	client: Apache common http://apache.org	Blocking	Library
		server : jetty embedded web server + servlet		
FTP	C/S	client : Apache-common-net/server:wu-ftpd	Blocking	Library
BitTorrent	P2P	BTPD http://btpd.sf.net	Non-Block	Daemon
S3	WAS	JetS3t https://jets3t.dev.java.net/	Blocking	Library
IBP	WAS	Java LoRS [BBF+02]	Non-Block	Library

searches and downloads. The DaemonConnector class acts as a wrapper around the P2P daemon and insures the start/stop of the daemon and the communications with the P2P daemon. Finally, it is sufficient to write 7 methods in the body of the Transfer class to integrate the new protocol: to *open* and *close* connection, to *probe* the end of transfer and to *send* and to *receive* file from the sender and the receiver peers.

Table 1 reports on the adaptability of the framework with a large variety of protocols and their implementation. Although not all of these back-ends would be stable enough to run in a production environment, these protocols have been successfully integrated into the framework, which demonstrate its versatility.

4.3 Asynchronous and Reliable File Transfers

Transfers are always initiated by a client host to the Data Transfer Service, which manages transfer reliability, resumes faulty transfers, reports on bytes transferred and ensures data integrity. Transfer management relies on a principle called *receiver driven transfer*. The sender of a datum periodically polls the receiver to check the progress of the transfer. Receiver detects the end of the transfer and check the integrity of the file by comparing the file size and the MD5 signature. This mechanism, while simple,

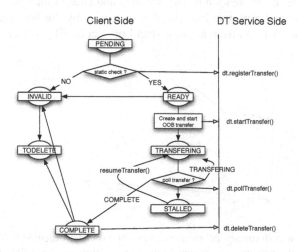

Fig. 3. Transfer transaction states and protocol between the client and the Data Transfer Service

ensures support for a broad range of different data transfer protocols in particular P2P
protocol. Indeed, in the case of P2P file transfer, the sender of a file cannot check by
itself whether a transfer is finished, because file recipient maybe have not received all
file chunks from other peers.

File transfer reliability is ensured by a protocol between the client and the Data
Transfer Service. Figure 3 presents the transfer transaction states and the protocol di-
alogues associated with transaction states. To start a file transfer, the client needs to
register the transfer on the DT Service side. All information needed to resume the file
transfer are stored in a stable memory, namely a SQL database. Therefore, in case of
crash of the client or DT service, the file transfer can be resumed from the last state
saved on the SQL database. Throughout the file transfer, client periodically poll DT to
obtain report on the transfer progress. This monitoring allows to detect stalled transfer
and to restart file transfer if the protocol permits it.

5   Performance Evaluation

In this section we report on performance evaluation in a Grid context, where experimental conditions are controlled and on the Internet to test our framework in real world
conditions. Experiments in our previous study [FHC08] have already evaluated the
overhead of BitDew when transferring data. We have observed a relatively low overhead (less than 8%) when transferring 500MB file to 250 nodes even under a stressful
configuration.

We have conducted our experiments in a Grid'5000 grid computing infrastructure
(see [Ba06] for more details). Grid'5000 is a nation wide Grid computing environment.

The first experiment evaluates the basic point-to-point data transfer performance.
The benchmark is a simple ping-pong, where a client creates a set of 1000 data of
varying size and registers this data on a Data Catalog. The set is then uploaded to a
Data Repository, monitored by a Data Transfer and downloaded back to the client. The
measurement starts at the creation of the first data and ends at the end of the last data
retrieval. Thus the entire protocol overhead is measured by the benchmark. Figure 4
presents the results with 3 different out-of-band protocols, FTP, HTTP or BitTorrent,

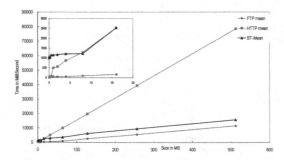

Fig. 4. Point-to-point performance comparison of the data transfer executed by FTP, HTTP and
BitTorrent. The curves present average transfer time in milliseconds for a file of a size varying
from 1KB to 512MB.

carrying on the file copy. The poor performance of HTTP can be explained by the use of an embedded Java web server (jetty) associated to a servlet to handle the file uploads.

In addition to our Grid'5000 testbed, we ran experiments using the Wide Area Storage offered by the Amazon S3 service and the IBP storage. Obviously, it was not possible to recreate the experimental condition of these file transfers within the Grid5000 infrastructure.

We measure the bandwidth from four different locations : a computer at LRI (Computer Science Laboratory) in Paris-Sud University (LRI), a PC at Knoxville connected to Internet by ISP cable at in Tennessee of USA (Knoxville), a server at Hohai University in Nanjing of China (Hohai), a computing node in Center for Computational Sciences of the University of Tsukuba, Japan (tsukuba). We then run bandwidth measurement by uploading and downloading 10 times files with three file sizes : 1, 10 and 100 MetaBytes. The DR and DT services run on a machine located at the LRI. This settings allowed us to confront our framework against a variety of settings from the point of view of the geography and the connectivity to Internet (ISP vs University backbone).

For IBP experiments, the list of L-Bone Server used are all in UTK campus: vertex.cs.utk.edu:6767 acre.sinrg.cs.utk.edu:6767 galapagos.cs.utk.edu:6767. All the duration of life of data is 24 hours. Each transfer uses only 1 connection, averaged 10 times. The data are sliced and transferred in 512k file chunks and stored on the following two depot servers : pound.cs.utk.edu:6714 and acre.cs.utk.edu:6714.

For Amazon S3 experiments, all the "buckets" are located in USA rather than Europe because of lower storage and transfer charges. In the site of Hohai University, the bandwidth of download is quite lower because of download limitation policy for international communications.

Table 2 and 3 presents the measurements.

We measure, on the LRI node, the duration of a ping-pong, performed each 15 minutes and the Figure 5 shows the cumulative distribution function (CDF) plot for the bandwidth obtained during the download and the upload of a 1MB file. Of course it is difficult to conclude about the performance as the experimental conditions may vary a lot.

Table 2. Measurements of IBP Protocol used by BitDew upload and download performance in KBytes/sec from different location on the Internet

Host	Location	Upload	Download
LRI	Orsay,France	126.54	198.52
Knoxville	Knoxville,TN,USA	44.50	545.98
Hohai	Nanjing,China	62.50	4.72
Tsukuba	Tsukuba,Japan	110.00	219.94

Table 3. Measurements of Amazon S3 used by BitDew upload and download performance in KBytes/sec from different location on the Internet

Host	Location	Upload	Download
LRI	Orsay,France	222.20	418.64
Knoxville	Knoxville,TN,USA	99.64	608.30
Hohai	Nanjing,China	34.87	2.50
Tsukuba	Tsukuba,Japan	113.85	238.82

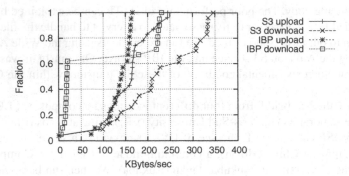

Fig. 5. Cumulative Distribution Function (CDF) plot

Results shows Overall, we can observe that those two "avant-garde" protocols for remote Internet storage are well integrated, and that it is possible to take advantage of these facilities.

6   Related Works

Collaborative Content Distribution is a very active research topic and several promising strategies [QS04] such as the use of network coding [GR05], are proposed to improve the performance of the system. Real life observation [IUKB+04] of a BitTorrent tracker during a five months period has shown the potential of this class of protocol : ability to serve large file to high number of nodes, resilience to flash-crowd effect, efficiency even in the context of high volatility, ability to serve file even if the original owner of the file has low bandwidth capacity. Oceanstore [Ka00], IBP [BBF+02], and Eternity [And96] aggregate a network of untrusted servers to provide global and persistent storage. IBP's strength relies on a comprehensive API to remotely store and move data from a set of well-defined servers. Using an IBP "storage in the network" service helps to build more efficient and reliable distributed application. Amazon S3 is a new class of Web Service offering Wide Area Storage. Two studies [Gar07, POIR07] have investigated the use of S3 for Grid Computing. With our service, one could use S3 and mix it with traditional or P2P approach to lower the cost of AS3.

7   Conclusion

We have proposed a multi-protocol file transfer service suitable for client/server and P2P protocols, as well as Wide Area Storage. Despite the fundamental differences between how file transfers are performed in this three classes of technologies, we have proposed a framework and mechanism (receiver-driven file transfer) which permit to encompass these protocols in an environment. Basic performance evaluation of our framework, both in a Grid context and on the Internet have shown the feasibility of our approach thanks to the high level features : asynchronism and reliability. This file transfer service can be useful for a large class of distributed applications : file sharing, remote backup, Grids etc.. First, it can serve as a multi-protocol file transfer library, featuring concurrent, reliable and P2P transfers. Second, it would be a means of leveraging future enhancements of P2P protocols and forthcoming WAS without modifying the distributed application.

References

[ama]   Amazon s3: Developer guide (March 2006)
[And96]   Anderson, R.: The eternity service. In: Proceedings of Pragocrypt 1996 (1996)
[aws]   Amazon web services
[Ba06]   Bolze, R., et al.: Grid5000: A large scale highly reconfigurable experimental grid
            testbed. International Journal on High Performance Computing and Applications
            (2006)
[BBF⁺02]   Bassi, A., Beck, M., Fagg, G., Moore, T., Plank, J.S., Swany, M., Wolski, R.: The
            Internet BackPlane Protocol: A Study in Resource Sharing. In: Second IEEE/ACM
            International Symposium on Cluster Computing and the Grid, Berlin, Germany
            (2002)
[Coh03]   Cohen, B.: Incentives Build Robustness in BitTorrent. In: Workshop on Economics
            of Peer-to-Peer Systems, Berkeley (2003)
[FHC08]   Fedak, G., He, H., Cappello, F.: BitDew: A Programmable Environment for Large-
            Scale Data Management and Distribution. Technical Report 6427, INRIA (January
            2008)
[FM06]   Fernandess, Y., Malkhi, D.: On Collaborative Content Distribution using Multi-
            Message Gossip. In: Proceeding of IEEE IPDPS, Rhodes Island (2006)
[Gar07]   Garfinkel, S.L.: An Evaluation of Amazon's Grid Computing Services: EC2, S3
            and SQS. Technical Report TR-08-07. Harvard University Cambridge, MA (2007)
[GR05]   Gkantsidis, C., Rodriguez, P.: Network Coding for Large Scale Content Distribu-
            tion. In: Proceedings of IEEE/INFOCOM 2005, Miami, USA (March 2005)
[IUKB⁺04]   Izal, M., Urvoy-Keller, G., Biersack, E.W., Felber, P.A., Hamra, A.A., Garces-
            Erice, L.: Dissecting BitTorrent: Five Months in a Torrent's Lifetime. In: Proceed-
            ings of Passive and Active Measurements (PAM) (2004)
[Ka00]   Kubiatowicz, J., et al.: OceanStore: An Architecture for Global-scale Persistent
            Storage. In: Proceedings of ACM ASPLOS. ACM, New York (2000)
[MM02]   Maymounkov, P., Mazières, D.: Kademlia: A Peer-to-peer Information System
            Based on the XOR Metric. In: Proceedings of the 1st International Workshop on
            Peer-to-Peer Systems (IPTPS 2002). MIT, Cambridge (2002)
[POIR07]   Palankar, M., Onibokun, A., Iamnitchi, A., Ripeanu, M.: Amazon S3 for Science
            Grids: a Viable Solution?. In: 4th USENIX Symposium on Networked Systems
            Design & Implementation (NSDI 2007) (2007)
[QS04]   Qiu, D., Srikant, R.: Modeling and Performance analysis of BitTorrent-like Peer-
            to-Peer Networks. SIGCOMM Comput. Commun. Rev. 34(4), 367–378 (2004)
[RD01]   Rowstron, A., Druschel, P.: Pastry: Scalable, distributed object location and rout-
            ing for large-scale peer-to-peer systems. In: IFIP/ACM International Conference
            on Distributed Systems Platforms (Middleware), Heidelberg, Germany (2001)
[SMK⁺01]   Stoica, I., Morris, R., Karger, D., Kaashoek, M.F., Balakrishnan, H.: Chord: A
            Scalable Peer-to-peer Lookup Service for Internet Applications. In: Proceedings
            of the ACM SIGCOMM 2001 Conference, San Diego, California (August 2001)

A Study of Reconstruction Process Load in P2P Storage Systems*

Ghislain Secret[1] and Gil Utard[2]

[1] LaRIA-MIS, Université de Picardie Jules Verne,
Amiens, France
[2] UbiStorage, Pôle Jules Verne,
Amiens, France

Abstract. In this paper we present a study of the load generated by the reconstruction process of P2P storage system. This reconstruction process maintains redundancy of data for durability to face peer failures found in P2P architectures. We will show that the cost induced is not negligible and we will show which parameters of the underlying P2P system can reduce it. To our best knowledge it is the first study of this topic.

1 Introduction

Today, Peer to Peer systems (P2P) are widely used mechanisms to share resources on Internet. Very popular systems were designed to share CPU (Seti@home, XtremWeb, Entropia) or to publish files (Napster, Gnutella, Kazaa). In the same time, some systems was designed to share disk space (OceanStore [4,9], Intermemory [2], PAST [3]. The primary goal of such systems is to provide a transparent distributed storage service. These systems share common issues with CPU or files sharing systems: resource discovery, localisation mechanisms, dynamic point to point network infrastructure... But for sharing disk systems data lifetime is the primary concern. P2P CPU or file publishing systems can deal with node failures: the computation can be restarted anywhere or the published files resubmitted to the system.

For disk sharing systems, node failure is a critical event: the stored data are definitively lost. So introducing data redundancy, such as the well known Rabin dispersal technique [5], and data recovery mechanisms is crucial for such systems.

Some previous works focused on the feasibility of such system, mainly for the data durability question: is the data redundancy scheme and data reconstruction mechanism sufficient to insure no data lost? Whereas the answer is yes for some parameters([1,10]), in [8], the authors outline that reconstruction processes introduce a new load in the P2P system, mainly the communication cost to maintain redundancy.

In this paper we present a first study of this load and the impact of the P2P system parameters on cost. This study is done by simulation. To our best

---

* This work is supported by the ANR Spreads project (www.spreads.fr).

A. Hameurlain (Ed.): Globe 2008, LNCS 5187, pp. 12–21, 2008.

knowledge it is the first work on this topic. After a presentation of usual redundancy schemes and reconstruction mechanisms used in P2P storage systems, we present our simulation process. We present the impact of system parameters on load induced by the reconstruction mechanism. Then we conclude.

2   Redundancy Scheme and Reconstruction Process

A peer-to-peer storage system is characterised by peers volatility. Peers connect and disconnect randomly. But in storage systems, the main issue is data durability. To cope with peers volatility, data redundancy is introduced.

The most simple method is data replication on different peers. To deal with r failures, data is replicated r times. However, replication requires a space r times larger than original data size. This ratio between the size of the data and actual space used to store the data is called *usable space*. Usable space is defined as the ratio between the original data size and the storage space. e.g.for a given 3 times replicated data, fault tolerance is 3 and useful space is $\frac{1}{1+r}$, i.e. $\frac{1}{4}$.

Storage systems that use replication as redundancy mechanism suffer from a low usable space. Other redundancy techniques that maximise usable space have been developed, like IDA schemes [5]. The mechanism is to fragment a data block in s fragments. Then, from these fragments, r redundancy fragments are computed. The $s + r$ fragments of the data block are distributed on different peers. Any combination of s fragments allows to rebuilt the raw data. Therefore the system tolerates r failures.

In the case of redundancy with fragmentation, usable space is expressed by the ratio $\frac{s}{s+r}$. e.g. for a given original data cut into 5 pieces, plus 3 redundancy fragments, fault tolerance is 3. Usable space is $\frac{s}{s+r}$, in our exemple: $\frac{5}{8}$. Blocks fragmentation allows usable space gain, for equivalent fault tolerance to replication. Therefore it allows to store more information in the system.

Note that replication is a special case of this redundancy scheme, where $s = 1$ and r is the number of replicates.

2.1   Reconstruction Process

In addition to redundancy scheme, a reconstruction mechanism of lost fragments is introduced to ensure data durability. A reconstruction threshold k is defined $(k \leq r)$. For each data block, when $r - k$ fragments are lost due to peer failures, a fragment regeneration process is triggered: $r - k$ alive peers will receive regenerated fragments. Note that it will be necessary to communicate the equivalent of the original data size (s fragments) through the system to conduct a reconstruction.

2.2   Reactivity Threshold

For a given block, k is the minimum redundancy fragments remaining in system before block reconstruction process is triggered. When redundancy fragments of a block is less than or equal than k, block rebuild process is launched to recover it. So, if $k = r - 1$, block reconstruction is initiated from the first fragment lost. We call this strategy *"anxious"*. At the opposite, if $k = 1$, block reconstruction is delayed until $r - 1$ fragments are lost, i.e. only one redundancy fragment remains in the network. This reconstruction strategy is called *"zen"*. Therefore k determines reactivity of the reconstruction process in the system.

These mechanisms allow data durability in network by judiciously setting system parameters. We refer to studies [6,8,7] to maintain data durability in P2P storage systems.

However, impact of system parameters on network load is not neutral. For each reconstruction, the block is communicated through the network. Hence, too often regenerate the redundancy of the system leads to a heavy load on the network. In this document, induced traffic (network load) in a P2P system is studied. It is the traffic generated by the permanent reconstructions, necessary to maintain data durability in system.

3   Peer to Peer Storage System Simulation

We consider a peer to peer storage system consisting of N independent peers who share their storage space. Peers are free to leave the system at any time. Peers who disappear are considered dead. It is assumed that the average population is constant, thus the average rate number of peers leaving the system is equal to the average rate number of peers who join it.

For the sake of simplicity, and without loss of generality, we consider that the data are blocks of uniform size.

A peer to peer storage system is determined by the parameters s, r and k, previously defined. We assume that the detection delay of a failed peer is constant. The regenerated fragments are randomly redistributed on living peers (which do not already have a fragment of the same block).

Peers lifetime is governed by a deviate law. Failure rate is determined by the number of peers in the network and their lifetime. For instance, in a 1,000 peers network, where the mean lifetime of each peer is 12 months, the average time between failures is 8 hours and 45 minutes. In this example there is about 3 failed peer per day.

Our study focuses on the data recovery costs in a peer to peer storage system, with the features set out above and without any data loss. We have developed a simulator to study the behaviour of the peer to peer storage system. The simulator evaluates the amount of data communicated between peers induced by the reconstruction process. The network load at time t is represented by the number of data blocks in a reconstruction state at time t.

Figure 1 shows an example of over time traffic load, in a 100 peers network, each storing 5 GB of data, and with a lifespan of 12 months. The block size is 10 MB. Each block is divided into 8 equally sized fragments, to which, using erasure codes, 8 redundancy fragments are added: $(s, r) = (8, 8)$. We assume that each peer is connected to the network through broadband connection (1 Mb download/256 Kb upload). The detection delay of peer failure is 1 day. The reconstruction threshold k is 5 remaining redundancy fragments.

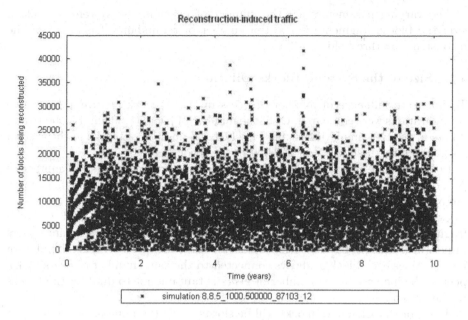

Fig. 1. Traffic load example

Figure 1 shows that reconstructions-induced traffic is not negligible. The average number of blocks being rebuilt is measured at each peer failure. For the parameters set in the simulation above, average blocks being rebuilt is 9216 blocks of a total of 500,000. The important standard deviation (5704) shows us significant variations in traffic load.

In this example, each peer hosts an average of 8,000 fragments, from various blocks. On average, 3 failed peers per day. This means that 24,000 fragments on average are lost every day. Among them, about 9000 blocks are critical (compared to k) and require a reconstruction.

The data volume exchanged between peers to rebuild the blocks is over than 100 GB a day, or more than 100 MB per peer and per day. Consequently, on average, each peer spends more than one hour per day for the reconstruction of the data. The volume of data exchanged to maintain the redundancy of data is important. It may reduce the bandwidth used by peers for data storage.

In the following, we will explore the factors which can reduce this traffic.

4   Parameters Effects

In this part, we will study influence of various system parameters on the reconstructions-induced load.

For all simulations, the following parameters are fixed. Each peer stores 5 GB of data. Data is divided into equally sized blocks. Each peer bandwidth is 256 Kb/s up and 1 Mb/s down. The simulation covers 10 years. The peer average lifetime is 12 months. The detection delay of a peer failure is one day.

The varying parameters are the number of peers in the system; the block size; the blocks fragmentation s; the number of redundancy fragments r; the reconstruction threshold k.

4.1   Size of the System, Blocks Dilution

To illustrate influence of number of peers in the network on traffic load, two configurations were compared. Only the number of peers (1,000 and 5,000 peers) differs in the two simulations exposed. The total number of blocks in the system is 50,000 in the first case and 250,000 in the second case.

In Figure 2, results show that network load is not proportional to number of peers. For instance in Figure 2, there is a factor 3 on the network load for a factor 5 on the number of peers.

Consider a block. If we increase the number of peers, the probability that a fragment of this block is located on a faulty peer is lower if there is more peers in network. This probability decreases faster than the increase of the number of blocks. Since each block is always connected to the same number of peers ($s + r$ peers), the increase in the number of peers is tantamount to diluting the blocks in the system.

Therefore, erosion data blocks will be slower when the number of peers in the system is greater. The need to rebuild appear later and, as a result, the network load on the reconstructions is reduced. Consequently large networks have a better performance in terms of network load on the storage volume available to the users.

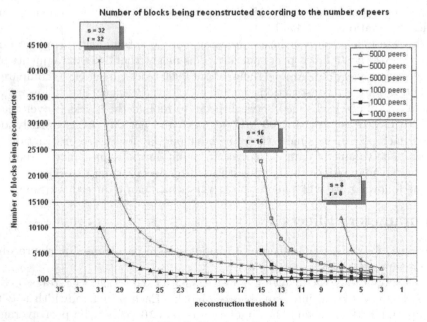

Fig. 2. Number of peers

4.2   System Reactivity

According to threshold k, network load evolution for different simulations is summarised in the Figure 3:

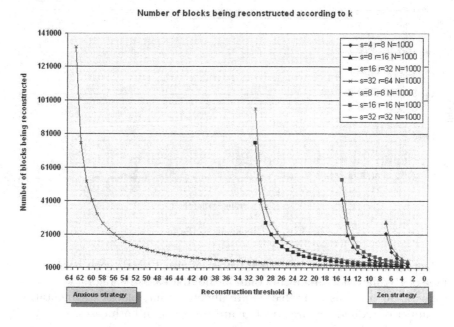

Fig. 3. Reactivity

Figure 3 shows that the gain in network load drop when reactivity k decreases by some units from the anxious strategy.

Therefore it is better to be not too anxious to reduce the network load of the system. Indeed, the gain on network load is on the first units of the reduction in the system reactivity. In fact, it is quite pointless to try to be as zen as possible. The gain on network load will be negligible. In addition, a too zen strategy might not allow the system to maintain data durability.

4.3   Data Dispersion

Data dispersion is defined by the ratio between number of blocks in network and number of peers. Note, with data volume per peer maintained constant, to increase the number of blocks in the system is to decrease the size of the blocks. In this case, peers host fragments of a larger number of blocks.

Two configurations were analysed, both in a 1,000 peers network: 50,000 blocks of size 100 MB each and 500,000 blocks of size 10 MB.

Increasing the block size from 10 to 100 MB leads to reduce the network load significantly (see Figure 4: an average of 8.5 times in this example), whatever the strategy implemented (regardless of the system reactivity k).

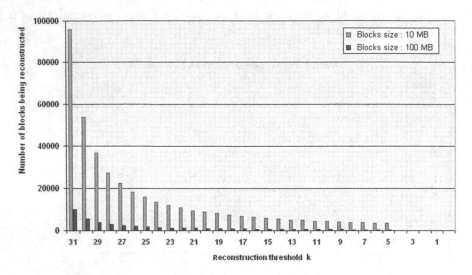

Fig. 4. Blocks size effects

In fact, in the second case (500,000 blocks of size 10 MB) each peer hosts an average of 10 times more fragments than in the first case. Therefore, when a peer disappears, 10 times as many blocks are affected. But, blocks fragmentation s and number of redundancy fragments r are the same in both cases. Probability that a given block is hit is greater, and as a result, it is necessary to rebuild more often.

When data volume is constant, increasing block size reduces the number of reconstructions. A larger block size allows to concentrate blocks on fewer peers.

However, when the block size increases, the fragments are also bigger. In our case, data volume exchanged in the reconstruction of each block is 10 times greater. During reconstruction, time required to transfer the fragments will be more important. However, this increase in time of reconstruction is negligible compared to time detection (of the order of one day).

4.4   Usable Space

Usable space is defined by the relationship between s and $s + r$. We will observe behaviour of the network load when parameters s and r vary. Two sets of simulations are conducted. In the first s is kept constant and the network load is measured with a value of r, then the double of that value. In the second, r is kept constant and the network load is measured with a value of s, then the double of that value.

When r is doubled, we see in the Figure 5 that the number of blocks being rebuilt is lower, regardless of the value of k.

For example, for $k = 20$, with $s = 32$ and $r = 32$, the average number of blocks being rebuilt is close to 9000. For the same value of $k = 20$ but with

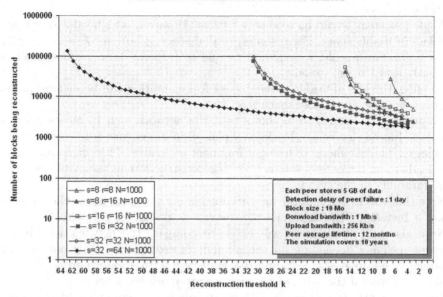

Fig. 5. Redundancy factor effects

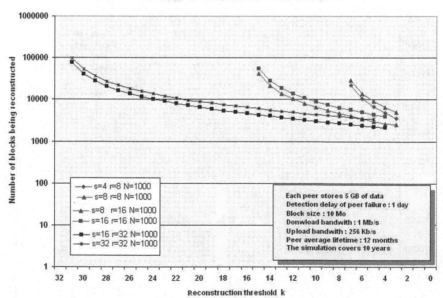

Fig. 6. Blocks segmentation effects

$s = 32$ and $r = 64$, the average number of blocks being rebuilt is close to 3000, i.e. three time less.

A good strategy would be to choose r great. However, a high value of r leads to a loss of usable space. For instance, usable space is 50% for $k = 20$, $s = 32$ and $r = 32$. For $k = 20$, $s = 32$ and $r = 64$ it drops to 33%. We operate less efficiently user storage space.

To offset the loss of usable space, blocks fragmentation can be increased, i.e. $s = 64$, $r = 64$, where usable space is 50%.

Unfortunately, the Figure 6 shows that the network load increases when s increases. Indeed, increasing blocks fragmentation in network is to expose more the blocks. The likelihood of losing a fragment is greater. That increase, therefore, leads to an increase in the number of reconstruction necessary to maintain data durability in the system.

Note that this increase in the network load is not proportional to the increase of s. For instance, it varies from +53% for $k = 5$ to +27% for $k = 31$.

Note also that the value k we choose to compare the network load has a different meaning depending on the number of redundancy fragments r. For instance, if the value of k is 15 and the value of r is 16, then we are in anxious strategy, whereas if the value of r is =32 we are much more zen.

Let δ be *anxiety level*, $\delta = \frac{k}{r-1}$. We can compare the number of blocks being rebuilt at a constant level of anxiety and constant usable space by setting $s = r$.

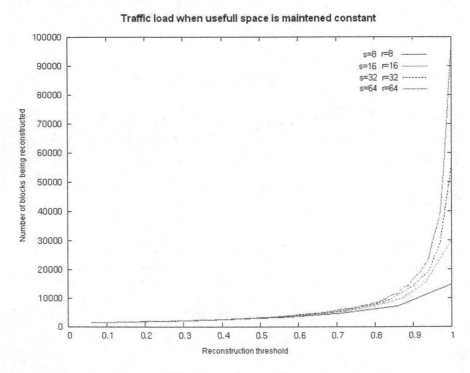

Fig. 7. s and r variations

Figure 7 shows the variation in the number of blocks being rebuilt under these conditions.

5   Conclusion

In this paper, we presented a study of the reconstruction process load in P2P storage system. Study was done by simulation of a generic P2P storage system. We shown this load is not negligible, so it is important to detect which parameters can reduce it. We shown that this load is proportional to the system size. We shown also that a too reactive system (say "anxious") generates huge load which can be significantly reduce by slightly diminishing reactivity of the reconstruction process, thus without compromising data durability of the system. We observed also that reducing spreading of data in the system reduce linearly the number of reconstruction but not the volume of data exchanged.

In this paper, we studied load for *reactive* system, that is regeneration of redundancy is done with a fixed threshold. As a future work, we plan to investigate the load in *pro-active* systems, when regeneration of redundancy is done preventively (using for instance information on age of peer).

References

1. Alouf, S., Dandoush, A., Nain, P.: Performance analysys of P2P storage systems. In: Mason, L.G., Drwiega, T., Yan, J. (eds.) ITC 2007. LNCS, vol. 4516. Springer, Heidelberg (2007)
2. Chen, Y., Edler, J., Goldberg, A., Gottlieb, A., Sobti, S., Yianilos, P.: A prototype implementation of archival intermemory. In: Proceedings of the Fourth ACM International Conference on Digital Libraries (1999)
3. Druschel, P., Rowstron, A.: PAST: A large-scale, persistent peer-to-peer storage utility. In: Procedings of HOTOS, pp. 75–80 (2001)
4. Kubiatowicz, J., Bindel, D., Chen, Y., Eaton, P., Geels, D., Gummadi, R., Rhea, S., Weatherspoon, H., Weimer, W., Wells, C., Zhao, B.: Oceanstore: An architecture for global-scale persistent storage. In: Proceedings of ACM ASPLOS. ACM, New York (2000)
5. Rabin, M.O.: Efficient dispersal of information for security, load balancing, and fault tolerance. J. ACM 36(2), 335–348 (1989)
6. Sit, E., Haeberlen, A., Dabek, F., Chun, B., Weatherspoon, H., Morris, R., Kaashoek, M., Kubiatowicz, J.: Proactive replication for data durability. In: 5th International Workshop on Peer-to-Peer Systems (IPTPS 2006). (2006)
7. Utard, G.: Perennite dans les systemes de stockage pair a pair. In: Ecole GRID 2002 (2002)
8. Utard, G., Vernois, A.: Data Durability in Peer-to-Peer Storage Systems. In: Proc. 4th Workshop on Global and Peer to Peer Computing. IEEE/ACM CCGrid Conference, Chicago (April 2004)
9. Wells, C.: The oceanstore archive: Goals, structures, and self-repair. Master's thesis. University of California, Berkeley (May 2001)
10. Williams, C., Huibonhoa, P., Holliday, J., Hospodor, A., Scwarz, T.: Redundancy management for p2p storage. In: Seventh IEEE International Symposium on Cluster Computing and The Grid (CCGrid 2007). IEEE, Los Alamitos (2007)

Subrange Caching: Handling Popular Range Queries in DHTs*

Marc Sànchez-Artigas[1], Pedro García-López[1], and Antonio G. Skarmeta[2]

[1] Universitat Rovira i Virgili, Catalonia, Spain
{marc.sanchez,pedro.garcia}@urv.cat
[2] Universidad de Murcia, Murcia, Spain
skarmeta@dif.um.es

Abstract. Range query, which is defined as retrieving all the keys within a certain range over the underlying DHT, has attracted a lot of attention recently. However, little has been done to speed up range queries through caching, one of the least studied P2P problems. In this paper, we present a caching protocol that (1) has excellent parallelizability, (2) can achieve $O(1)$ complexity for moderate range queries, and (3) balances the access load among all the DHT peers. Our experimental results shows significant gains in both range query performance and load balancing, with minimal overhead.

1 Introduction

Structured Peer-to-Peer (P2P) systems have built overlay networks by organising nodes in prefixed topologies in the provision of large-scale, decentralised routing platforms. Different structures have been proposed, the most popular of which are Distributed Hash Tables (DHTs), such as CAN [1] and Chord [2], to name a few. DHTs support "exact-match" queries efficiently through consistent hashing, but require specific mechanisms to support complex queries, as hashing destroys the semantic relation between the keys. As a result, DHTs do not support directly complex queries based on the ordering of keys, which includes range queries. To deal with this problem, several solutions has been proposed that claim to support range queries very efficiently. However, little had been done on the development of caching algorithms that improve range query search and its relationship with access load balancing. Many of the existing solutions are based on data migration which is rather inadequate to support skewed access distributions. This becomes more apparent in the case of a single popular range which makes all the nodes that lie in it heavily loaded. Transferring the keys in the range to the neighboring peers only transfers the problem. For that reason, it is important to develop new protocols that decrease the ocurrence of hot-spots in the network.

In this paper, we take a further step and develop a caching protocol for range queries which leads to a fair distribution of load over the nodes in the network. To

---

* This research was partially funded through project P2PGRID, TIN2007-68050-C03-03, of the Ministry of Education and Science, Spain.

A. Hameurlain (Ed.): Globe 2008, LNCS 5187, pp. 22–33, 2008.

meet this goal, our protocol caches range queries "on the fly", setting up pointers to the peers that (recently) requested a certain range, rather than replicating the whole range elsewhere. Given a range query $[l, u]$, where l and u denote the *lower bound* and *upper bound* resp., the key idea is that each peer in $[l, u]$ that processes the query enters a pointer in its cache to the querying peer. This way a future query will be partially or totally answered by redirecting the query peer to the peers that recently downloaded a subrange of $[l, u]$. In particular, we make the following contributions:

1. A novel protocol for caching range queries over DHTs that, besides handling uneven key distributions, balances access load among peers when ranges are accessed with different frequency, for example, due to a Zipf distribution. Its main features are the following: (1) it possesses excellent parallelizability, (2) it can achieve O(1) complexity for moderate queries, (3) it balances the access load among all the DHT peers, and (4) it can be applied to many DHTs with slight modifications (we use Chord for our examples and experiments).
2. The results from experimentation illustrate that our caching protocol achieves its main goals: a significant reduction in terms of hop counts per range query, from 30% to 80% compared with Chord, and a fair distribution of load.

To our knowledge, this is the first work to concurrently address caching and access load balancing in DHTs, studying in detail its performance features.

In the following section, we discuss related work. In section 3, we explain our protocol in detail. Experimental results are presented in section 4. Finally, we conclude this work in section 5.

2 Related Work

Although there exists a large body of literature in range queries, there has been little examination of the use of caching to improve range query searches. Some indicative examples are the works of Khotari et al. [3] and Sahin et al. [4], from University of California, Santa Barbara.

In [3], the authors present a P2P architecture over Chord that allows to cache range queries as they are executed. Their solution uses a hash function based on min-wise independent permutations, but it can only supply approximate answers to the queries. In contrast, our caching protocol ensures completeness.

The authors of [4] extend CAN [1] to decrease the burden of answering range queries from a single data source. However, their architecture has two important shortcomings. First, its performance is inferior to our solution, as searches require $O(2n^{1/2})$ hops. Second, the nodes at the upper-left region of the CAN's virtual space are heavily loaded, since, by construction, they store the largest ranges.

Finally, it is worth mentioning the work of Pitoura et al. [5] which strives to address simultaneously the problem of providing efficient range query processing and access load balancing. Their solution uses a novel locality-preserving hash function, and a tunable replication algorithm that trades off replication overhead for a fair load distribution. However, their solution incurs a large amount of hops, even for moderate range sizes, because they do not cache popular ranges.

3   Subrange Caching

This section describes our caching protocol. First, we delve into the problem we address in this paper. Then, we present how answers are cached at peers and are used for answering future range queries.

3.1   Problem Definition

As a primary goal, DHTs has devoted a lot of efforts to achieve efficiency in key lookups, typically at $O(\log n)$ complexity. However, the inherent *exact maching* in DHT lookup protocols has restricted DHT applicability only to simple queries. Complex queries, such as range queries, are difficult to achieve directly, because the cryptographic hash function they use to balance load (e.g., SHA-1) destroys the locality of keys.

To preserve the ordering of keys, we use a locality-preserving hash function, a common practice to support range queries over DHTs. To illustrate, consider that $D_\alpha = [l_\alpha, u_\alpha]$ is the domain for a numeric attribute α. We define a locality preserving hash function, h, for α as $h(x) : D_\alpha \rightarrow \{0, 1, 2, ..., 2^m - 1\}$ such that if $x < y$, then $h(x) < h(y)$, $\forall x, y \in \{0, 1, 2, ..., 2^m - 1\}$, where m specifies the size of the underlying DHT key space.

However, this additional capability comes at a price: preserving key locality can cause load imbalances at two levels: (1) at the key-assignment level, because the skewed distribution of attribute values can lead to assign a disproportionate number of keys to some peers; and (2) at the query level (access of keys). While there are many papers that deal with the first problem, what is still lacking is a framework that, besides achieving $O(1)$ complexity for range queries, can handle skewed access distributions. One way of doing this is through caching. However, not all caching implementations are equally valid. For example, a naïve solution would be to maintain an *inverted index* of which nodes have cached each range. Using the underlying DHT logic, the index for a range $[l, u]$ could be kept at the peer responsible for the SHA-1 hash of $[l, u]$. In this way, information about who caches $[l, u]$ would be accessible by each peer in the DHT via a lookup operation.

This approach although simple, only supports range lookup for exact matches. However, even if the requested range $[l, u]$ does not exist, there may be another range $[l - \xi, u + \xi']$ which could have easily satisfied the query. Or, one may join multiple smaller partitions to expand $[l, u]$. Finding such partitions is the main challenge of this paper.

With the above in mind, the problem we solve can be stated in the following way:

Definition 1. *(The Range Query Caching Problem): Given a range query $[l, u]$, locate one or more peers so that*

1. *The union of all the subranges they possess expands* $[l, u]$;
2. *No peer is heavily overloaded; and*
3. *Range query complexity is* $O(1)$.

Before proceeding any further, we would like to list the assupmtions we make in this work:

1. The number of of keys a peer is responsible for is already balanced. This can be done either by making use of a *uniform* locality-preserving hash function (see [6]) or by adapting the DHT topology to the *non-uniform* distribution of keys (see [7]); and
2. The DHT itself does not introduce systematic hot-spots due to variations in the *in-degree* and *out-degree* distributions at each peer.

The second assumption is important to ensure that our results are not biased. Upon arrival, a joining peer has to be assigned an ID from the key space. Early DHT designs such as Chord allowed each peer to independently choose a number in $\{0, 1, 2, ..., 2^m - 1\}$ uniformly at random, dividing the circumference $[0, 2^m)$ into a sequence of disjoint arcs. The consequence of this is that some peers has an in-degree of $O(\log^2 n)$ w.h.p. instead of $O(\log n)$, which increases the inequality in the load distribution. This happens whenever a peer p has not other peers in the range $[p - 2^n(\log n)/n, p]$, because then p attracts an average number of $\log n$ other peers for each distance 2^i, resulting in $O(\log^2 n)$ incoming links w.h.p. For this reason, throughout the paper, we assume that the *in-degree* and *out-degree* of all Chord nodes is $\Theta(\log n)$.

3.2   Design of Subrange Caching

In this section, we describe the main components that integrate subrange caching. Nodes running the *Subrange Caching* (SC) protocol maintain a *range cache*, or a list of pointers to other nodes, that is used to temporarily maintain references to the peers that have (recently) sought for a certain range. To meet this goal, the range cache is accompanied by a set of rules. The most important, the *insertion rule*, is a follows. For clarity, let us denote the identity of a peer p by $p.id$. Then,

Definition 2. *(Insertion rule): Given a range query* $[l, u]$ *and a query peer* q, *a peer* p *can set up a pointer to* q *if* $p.id \in [l, u]$.

What the above rules states is that only the peers located within range $[l, u]$ can store pointers in its cache. The purpose is to overlap range query processing with caching in such a fashion that while the query is being processed, whenever a peer p knows about other peers that have recently downloaded some subrange of $[l, u]$, p returns the reference to these peers rather than sending its keys. This ensures that range queries are "correct" with no additional communication. That is, if a peer does not find any subrange in its cache, it merely appends the keys it is responsible of to the answer and continues the query. This is advantageous for two reasons:

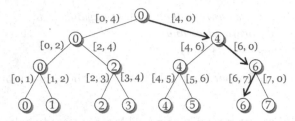

Fig. 1. Partitioning of the key space induced by Chord routing geometry

1. In the worst case, the communication cost incurred by SC equals to the cost of processing the range query; and
2. The correctness of the query is independent of the number of parts currently cached at the peers. Only search complexity is affected by the fact that only 1, 2 or n parts of the query are in the cache: The less the number of cached parts, the more the number of forwardings (hops). So as long as the span of queried range is moderate, $O(1)$ complexity for range query can be achieved, as demonstrated in Section 4.

By correctness, we mean the following:

Definition 3. *(Correctness): Given a range query $[l, u]$, a set R of ranges $[l_i, u_i]$ is a correct query result for $[l, u]$ if the following two conditions hold:*

1. *$[l_i, u_i] \cap [l_j, u_j] = \emptyset$ when $i \neq j$; and*
2. *The union of all ranges $[l_i, u_i] \in R$ expand $[l, u]$.*

Once defined the notion of correctness for query results, we are now ready to explain the relation between the above two definitions. Before going any further, we believe convenient to illustrate how SC works. Given a range $[l, u]$, it consists of two steps:

1. Routing to the node responsible of l (using the underlying DHT logic); and
2. Processing the range query concurrently, with the peers forwarding the query to their neighbors only in $[l, u]$, until the union of their subranges can satisfy the query. At the extreme case, where every peer has not an entry to satisfy $[l, u]$, each peer returns the keys it owns, as in a standard range query.

With the above in mind, it is evident that an answer to a range query consists of a sequence of subranges $[l_i, u_i]$, some cached, others not, that must be retrieved without affecting the correctness of the query. In order to do this, we exploit the "natural" partitioning of the key space that arises in the routing geometries of DHTs.

Key Space Partitioning. By the examination of the DHTs that have $O(\log n)$ complexity such as Chord, Symphony [8], and Kademlia [9], one can easily note that the basic principle behind their operation consists in performing a form of recursive search in which at each step, the distance to the destination decreases exponentially. In the case of Chord, this corresponds to *binary search*. Hence, the distance to the destination is halved at each forwarding. This induces a natural partition on the key space (in form of a binary tree) that allows to view the key space as sequence of telescoping partitions. For other DHTs, what varies is the tree arity, but the same arguments follow.

In what follows, we explain the perception of Chord a sequence of partitions that are structured in form of a tree.

We assume the familiarity of the reader to Chord and its terminology. Like in any DHT, Chord is characterized by the routing tables employed at each node. Let k denote the size of the routing table at each node. At a node of identification id, the ith entry in the table contains the identity of the first node that succeeds id by at least 2^{i-1} on the key space $[0, 2^m)$. We call this node the ith finger of the node, and denote it by $id.finger[i]$. The routing algorithm is simply as follows: Forward a request for key β to node $id.finger[i]$ if $\beta - id \in S_i = [2^{i-1}, 2^i)$. For correctness of routing, $S_i \cap S_j = \emptyset$ when $i \neq j$. The consequence of this is that at each node, the key space is partitioned into disjoint subranges of exponentially increasing size. For a node with identifier id, the set of partitions is the following: $[id, id+1)$, $[id+1, id+2)$, ..., $[id+2^{m-1}, id+2^m)$, all arithmetic modulo 2^m. An example to clarify this point is presented below.

Assume that all positions of a Chord network of size $n = 2^{m=3}$ are occupied by live peers. In Figure 1, we show the binary search tree of a lookup originating at peer 0. The ranges above the arcs illustrate how the key space, i.e., $[0, 7)$, is recursively partitioned from the root (peer 0) to the leaves. To better understand this, consider that peer 0 issues a query for key $\beta = 6$. Initially, the entire key space is considered for the search. Based on the range to which the key belongs, the query is then forwarded to the *left* or the *right* child. Since $\beta = 6$ belongs to $[4, 7)$, peer 0 forwards the query to peer 4. Then peer 4 repeats the same process but with the search space reduced to a half of the previous space. As a result, peer 4 forwards the query to peer 6. Since peer 6 is the peer responsible of range $[6, 7)$, the query terminates. One important consequence of this is that all peers are reachable after $O(\log_2 n)$ forwardings, since $\log_2 2^{m=3} = 3$ is the maximum height of the tree.

However, the key observation is the following: Since Chord routing geometry defines a *full binary tree* rooted at each peer, it is trivial to verify that any range query can be represented by a union of some intervals on the tree. For instance, the range query $[2, 6]$ can be represented by the union of the intervals $[2, 4)$, $[4, 6)$ and $[6, 7)$, as shown in Figure 1. This leads to the following theorem.

Theorem 1. *Given a peer p, any range $R = [u, l]$ can be represented by a union of some intervals on the routing tree rooted at p. Furthermore, there exist multiple possible unions for any range R with length > 1, all correct, when R is processed according to standard Chord routing.*

Proof. Due to the space limitation, we only give a short proof of the second half of the theorem. Each non-leaf node a on the binary tree has two children. A left child and a right child that represent the intervals $\left[a.id, succ\left(a.id + 2^{m-(d(a)+1)}\right)\right)$

and $\left[succ \left(a.id + 2^{m-(d(a)+1)} \right), a.id \right)$, respectively, where $d(a)$ denotes the depth of node a on the tree, $d(a) \in [0, m-1]$. The union of the two children covers the same interval as the parent does. So, for any range of length > 1, there exist at least two possibilities to cover (part of) this range: The union of the two children intervals or the parent range. This concludes the first part. Since standard Chord routing splits the remaining range into two disjoint intervals at each forwarding, the resultant intervals are always disjoint. Hence, its union correct.   □

Although there are multiple possibilities to represent a large range with the union of smaller subranges, it is clear that larger subranges, if cached, incur less communication. For instance, following the above example, if interval $[2, 4)$ was in the cache of peer 2, jumping to peer 3 could be skipped, incurring 1 hop less.

Range Cache. Having highlighted the idea of the natural partitioning that lies at the heart of routing algorithms, we now describe how references are organized into the range cache. For a range query $[l, u]$, let $q([l, u])$ be the node that wishes to search range $[l, u]$. To simplify exposition, suppose that a peer p with $p.id$ in $[l, u]$ receives a query for this partition. As specified by the insertion rule, peer p is allowed to enter a pointer to $q([l, u])$ in its cache. However, the question we address here is how to maintain the pointer to $q([l, u])$ in the cache so that access load is minimized. By maintaning only the pointers corresponding to the largest ranges, p will maximize the number of hits. However, it will worsen access load balancing, since the number of peers that will retrieve large ranges is expected to be low (due to bandwidth constraints). To optimize both properties, we organize the pointers into the cache according to the partitioning of the key space induced by the fingers. In particular, we organize the range cache in k levels (in a similar way to the finger table). Then, we apply the following rule upon a new insertion:

Definition 4. *(Placement rule) Given a range $[l, u]$ and a peer p, range $[l, u]$ is assigned to level i, $1 \le i \le m$, if*

1. *p verifies the insertion rule; and*
2. *i is the smallest integer such that $p.finger[i].id \in (p.id, u)$, i.e., the largest partition of the form $[p.id, p.finger[i].id)$ contained in $[l, u]$.*

In this way, we can classify queries by the size of their ranges, and redirect the querying peer to the member whose cached range *approximates* the most the range of its query. Since ranges are variable in size, it can be easily seen that the placement rule will translate such diversity into a source of load balancing. To better understand this, turn attention to the example in Figure 1. Due to space limitations, we only describe the effect of the placement rule upon peer 0. Now, consider two ranges queries, $R_1 = [0, 3]$ and $R_2 = [0, 6]$, resp. According to this rule, peer 0 will cache R_1 at level 1 and R_2 at level 2, respectively. Thus, range query $[0, 4]$ will be answered by R_1 + a jump to peer 4, thereby off-loading $q(R_2)$ from the burden of answering all the ranges due to it downloaded a large range. The negative effect is that this query is split into two new queries over the two children intervals $[0, 4)$ and $[4, 0)$, which, fortunately, can be executed in parallel.

Clearly, this rule achieves a better trade-off between load and performance, but does not affect the correctness of the query.

Because peers in P2P systems typically exhibit short lifetimes, references may lead to dead peers, which can result in poor query performance. To counter this problem, it is necessary to ensure that entries are fresh. This can be accomplished by periodically selecting an entry and sending a *ping* message to it. Notice that once the bandwidth consumption for maintenance is fixed, the rate at which an entry is checked is inversely proportional to the size of the cache. Therefore, it is important that the cache is not too large; otherwise, it cannot be "properly" maintained. To limit the maintenance cost of the cache, we impose a threshold, we call it s, on the number of cache entries per level.

Another factor that affects load balancing is the cache replacement policy. A cache replacement policy determines what entries to be evicted from the cache. Therefore, a policy that prioritizes entries with the most recent timestamps may lead to a poor balancing of load, since accesses will be concentrated on the most recently used (MRU) peers. To ensure fairness, we choose cache entries uniformly at random (RAN), which maximizes load balancing.

Theorem 2. *Given a set of s entries, the expected number of cache replacements to evict all these entries using the RAN policy is $s \ln s + O(s)$.*

Proof. The probability of evicting 1 of the s entries from the cache only changes after a new initial entry is evicted. While waiting for evicting the ith entry (after having evicted $(i-1)$ old entries) the probability of eviction is $p_i = 1 - \frac{(i-1)}{s}$. Let X_i be the waiting time between evicting the $(i-1)^{th}$ and i^{th} entries. Clearly, X_i is geometrically distributed. As such, $E[X_i] = \frac{1}{p_i}$. Let X be the number of entries evicted until all the initial s entries have been removed from the cache. Clearly, $X = \sum_{i=1}^{s} X_i$. Therefore, $E[X] = E\left[\sum_{i=1}^{s} X_i\right] = \sum_{i=1}^{s} E[X_i] = \sum_{i=1}^{s} \frac{s}{(s-i+1)} = s \ln s + O(s)$, and the lemma follows. $\qquad\qquad\square$

Consequently, after $s \ln s + O(s)$ replacements, all the initial entries are evicted, thereby balancing the access load across all peers in the system.

3.3 Query Processing

Algorithm 1 and 2 give the pseudocode for our range query caching protocol. Remote calls are preceded by the peer identifier. Thus, $p.\text{Foo}()$ denotes a *remote procedure call* to peer p. References to variables are local to the peers.

For a querying peer p and a range query $[l, u]$, INITRANGEQUERY() returns a *correct* query result, R, that satisfies $[l, u]$. Initially, p invokes FINDSUCCESSOR() (Chord lookup algorithm) using l as key, and the query is forwarded to the node, p', responsible of l. Then, p' lookups it cache. If it has a superrange of $[l, u]$, the query finishes. Otherwise, p' appends the reference to the largest subrange it has in its cache to R in order to minimize the number of query forwardings. Suppose that this range is $[l_i, u_i]$. In order to ensure correctness, observe that p' may need to trim $[a, b]$ to $[p'.id, p'.finger[j].id - 1]$, where j is the level at where $[a, b]$ was

---

Algorithm 1. $p.\text{INITRANGEQUERY}([l, u], R)$

1: $p' = p.\text{FINDSUCCESSOR}(p.id)$
2: $j, ref = p'.\text{LOOKUPCACHE}([l, u])$.
3: **if** $[l, u] \subset ref.range$ **then**
4:    **return** $R = R \cup \{ref\}$
5: **end if**
6: **for** $i = j$ to $m - 1$ **do**
7:    **if** $p'.finger[i].id \neq p'.finger[i + 1].id$ **then**
8:       **if** $p'.finger[i + 1].id \in (p'.id, u)$ **then**
9:          $limit = p'.finger[i + 1].id$
10:       **else**
11:          $limit = u$
12:       **end if**
13:       $R = R \cup p'.finger[i].\text{FINDSUBRANGE}(limit, [l, u], p, R)$
14:    **end if**
15: **end for**
16: **if** $p'.finger[m - 1].id, p'.id, u)$ **then**
17:    $R = R \cup p'.finger[m - 1].\text{FINDSUBRANGE}(u, [l, u], p, R)$
18: **end if**
19: $p'.\text{INSERTRANGEINTOCACHE}([l, u], p)$
20: **return** R

Algorithm 2. $p.\text{FINDSUBRANGE}(limit, [l, u], q, R)$

1: $j, ref = p.\text{LOOKUPCACHE}([l, u])$.
2: $R = R \cup \{ref\}$
3: **for** $i = j$ to $m - 1$ **do**
4:    **if** $p.finger[i].id \neq p.finger[i + 1].id$ **then**
5:       **if** $p.finger[i].id \in (p.id, limit)$ **then**
6:          **if** $p.finger[i + 1].id \in (p.id, limit)$ **then**
7:             $newLimit = p.finger[i + 1].id$
8:          **else**
9:             $newLimit = limit$
10:          **end if**
11:          $R = R \cup p.finger[i].\text{FINDSUBRANGE}(newLimit, [l, u], q, R)$
12:       **end if**
13:    **end if**
14: **end for**
15: $p.\text{INSERTRANGEINTOCACHE}([l, u], q)$
16: **return** R

---

found. The reason for this is to ensure that the ranges requested to the reference peers are *pairwise disjoint*, so that each key is sent to p exactly once.

After skipping the redundant fingers, p' forwards the query to every finger $p.finger[i]$, $j \leq i < m$, whose id is before u. A variable called $limit$ is used to restrict the fowarding space of the receiving peers. The $limit$ of $p'.finger[i].id$ is $p'.finger[i + 1].id$, $1 \leq i < m$.

A node p receiving a RPC for $\text{FINDSUBRANGE}(limit, [l, u], q, R)$ continues the range query processing in the subtree covered by partition $(p.id, limit)$. Besides skipping the redundant fingers, p lookups its cache for a range that satisfies $[l, u]$ (if any), and forwards the query to every finger $p.finger[i]$, $j \leq i < m$, whose id is before the $limit$. Moreover, when forwarding the query to any finger, p supplies it with a $newLimit \in (p.id, limit)$ to ensure that: (1) There is no redundancy, i.e., every peer in $[l, u]$ receives the request exactly once; and (2) The subranges kept at the reference peers are non-overlapping in order to obtain a correct query result (see definition 3).

At this point, it must be noted that both algorithms are parallelizable at the **for** loop, since calls to FINDSUBRANGE() can be done in parallel with no risk of losing correctness on results. The *limit* parameters controls this. Hence, as long as the span of queried range is moderate, O(1) complexity can be achieved, as demonstrated in the next section.

4   Experimental Evaluation

In this section, we evaluate SC. As a baseline for the evaluation, we use a locality preserving Chord network [10] we simply term Chord. To generate a range query $[l, u]$, we select a key β uniformly at random to be the middle point of the range, and then, we compute the upper and lower bounds as follows: $[\lfloor \beta - \frac{\delta}{2} \rfloor, \lfloor \beta + \frac{\delta}{2} \rfloor]$, where $\delta \sim N(\mu = 250, \sigma = 75)$ (normally distributed). In order to model skewed access patterns, we use a Zipf distribution over 1K midpoints. Recall that in Zipf distributions, the number of queries for the ith most popular item is proportional to $i^{-\rho}$, where ρ is as positive constant. For all the experiments, we set $\rho = 0.85$, a typical value found in the literature. Also, we use a key space of size 2^{15} and perform $n_q = 20$K queries per experiment. Unless otherwise noted, the number of peers is $n = 4000$. The results are shown in terms of: (1) Efficiency in query processing: mainly measured in terms of number of hops and key-hit ratio. Key-hit ratio represents the fraction of keys that has been retrieved from caches; and (2) Access load balancing: in terms of Lorenz curves and Gini coefficient.

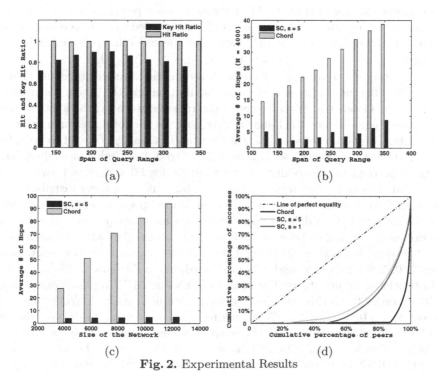

(a)

(b)

(c)

(d)

Fig. 2. Experimental Results

Efficiency in query processing. In this experiment, we inject into the network the same set of $n_q = 2K$ ranges queries in both systems and measure the number of hops required to satisfy them. Since both algorithms initially route to the lower bound l of a range query, we focus here on the number of hops needed to complete a query once l is reached. Figure 2b shows how the average hop-count varies against the query span. While Chord incurs more hops as the query span enlarges, SC's average hop-count stabilizes around 7, which proves that SC expends at most $O(1)$ routing hops, irrespective of the query span.

Figure 2c depicts the comparison results between SC and Chord, as network size increases from 4K to 12K. Comparing SC against Chord, we can conclude, as expected, that SC achieves significant hop-count savings that are more prominent as the network size increases. Finally, Figure 2a illustrates the hit ratio and key-hit ratio for SC($s = 5$). Clearly, they explain the great savings achieved by SC in the mean hop-count: a key-hit ratio that does not go below 80% for all ranges.

Access Load Balancing. Lorenz curves and the Gini coefficient are widely used in economics to estimate income inequality. In this work, we use these two metrics to estimate the distribution of access load. More specifically, the Lorenz curve is a ranked distribution of the cumulative percentage of individuals on the abcissa versus the cumulative percentage of load (number of accesses) along the ordinate axis. The greater the distance this curve is from the diagonal line, called the *line of equality*, the greater the inequality in load. That is, if all peers have the same load, the curve is a straight diagonal line, whereas if there exists some imbalance, it falls below the line of equality. More formally, for a population of size n, with a sequence of load values l_i, $\forall i = 1..n$, which are indexed in non-decreasing order ($l_i \leq l_{i+1}$), the Lorenz curve is the continuous piecewise linear function joining the points ($\frac{i}{n}, \frac{L_i}{L_n}$), $\forall i = 0..n$, where $L_0 = 0$, and $L_i = \sum_{j=1}^{i} l_j$.

On the other hand, the Gini coefficient is a numeric measure of inequality that reveals the difference between a uniform distribution and the actual distribution of a resource. Geometrically, it expresses the ratio between (a) the area enclosed by the line of equality and the Lorentz curve, and (b) the total area under the line of equality. The Gini coefficient ranges from *perfect equity* ($G = 0$) to *complete inequity* ($G = 1$). Therefore, as G comes closer to 0, load imbalances diminish.

Figure 2d depicts the resulting Lorenz curves for SC with $s = 1$ and $s = 5$, and Chord. As can be seen from thes picture, SC achieves a fairer distribution of load than Chord, with the top 10% heaviest-loaded peers receiving about 50% fewer accesses than Chord. These positive results are consequence of the random selection of the reference peers at each level in conjunction with the placement rule. The same behavior is observed if we take into account the Gini coefficient, which is 0.72 for SC($s = 5$) and 0.96 for Chord, i.e., a decrease of 25%.

To conclude, we investigate the effect of RAN and MRU replacement policies on SC. In order to do this, in this experiment, we limit cache lookups to a level at most k_{max}, $0 \leq k_{max} < k$. With this test, what we want to examine is how load balancing degrades when the large-span ranges are necessarily answered by the pointers at level k_{max}. Table 1 shows the results. As can be seen, MRU is worse than RAN in all properties, which suggests that randomness is critical to

Table 1. The effect of k_{max} on RAN and MRU replacement policies

k_{max}	Gini Coefficient		Max. Load (% of total)		Average # of Hops	
	RAN	MRU	RAN	MRU	RAN	MRU
7	0.69	0.93	43%	47%	14.04	15.17
8	0.68	0.90	15%	17%	7.82	8.55
9	0.67	0.84	3%	6%	3.62	3.92

balance load. Moreover, as k_{max} diminishes, the load imposed on the heaviest-loaded increases, which indicates that as much variability in the cache, the less the load imposed on the most accessed peers.

5   Conclusions

In this paper, we have presented a caching protocol aimed at accelerating range queries over DHTs, one of the least studied research problems in DHTs. Its main feature is that it exploits the key space partitioning induced by standard routing algorithms to achieve $O(1)$ complexity for moderate range queries, while balancing access load among all the peers in the system. Simulation results verify our thesis, and show significant gains in the above two properties.

References

1. Ratnasamy, S., Francis, P., Handley, M., Karp, R., Schenker, S.: A scalable content-addressable network. In: SIGCOMM 2001, pp. 161–172 (2001)
2. Stoica, I., et al.: Chord: a scalable peer-to-peer lookup protocol for internet applications. IEEE/ACM Trans. Netw. 11(1), 17–32 (2003)
3. Kothari, A., Agrawal, D., Gupta, A., Suri, S.: Range addressable network: A p2p cache architecture for data ranges. In: P2P 2003 (2003)
4. Sahin, O.D., Gupta, A., Agrawal, D., Abbadi, A.E.: A peer-to-peer framework for caching range queries. In: ICDE 2004, pp. 165–177 (2004)
5. Pitoura, T., Ntarmos, N., Triantafillou, P.: Replication, load balancing and efficient range query processing in dhts. In: Grust, T., Höpfner, H., Illarramendi, A., Jablonski, S., Mesiti, M., Müller, S., Patranjan, P.-L., Sattler, K.-U., Spiliopoulou, M., Wijsen, J. (eds.) EDBT 2006. LNCS, vol. 4254, pp. 131–148. Springer, Heidelberg (2006)
6. Cai, M., Frank, M., Chen, J., Szekely, P.: Maan: A multi-attribute addressable network for grid information services. In: GRID 2003, pp. 184–192 (2003)
7. Girdzijauskas, S., Datta, A., Aberer, K.: On small world graphs in non-uniformly distributed key spaces. In: ICDEW 2005, p. 1187 (2005)
8. Manku, G., Bawa, M., Raghavan, P.: Symphony: Distributed hashing in a small world. In: USITS 2003 (2003)
9. Maymounkov, P., Mazieres, D.: Kademlia: A peer-to-peer information system based on the xor metric. In: Druschel, P., Kaashoek, M.F., Rowstron, A. (eds.) IPTPS 2002. LNCS, vol. 2429. Springer, Heidelberg (2002)
10. Triantafillou, P., Pitoura, T.: Towards a unifying framework for complex query processing over structured peer-to-peer data networks. In: DBISP2P 2003, p. 169 (2003)

Context-Aware Cache Management in Grid Middleware

Fabrice Jouanot, Laurent d'Orazio, and Claudia Roncancio

Grenoble Informatics Laboratory, France
firstname.lastname@imag.fr

Abstract. This paper focuses on context-aware data management services in grids with the aim of constructing self-adaptive middleware. The contribution is twofold. First it proposes a framework to facilitate the development of context management services. The reason is that, even a context management service, is context specific. The creation of ad-hoc context managers is crucial. Second, this papers introduces context awareness in cooperative semantic caches. Preliminary results of our experiments on the Grid5000 platform are reported.

1 Introduction

Large scale distributed systems as, Grids and P2P systems, facilitate resource sharing among numerous and heterogeneous sites and participants. Supporting appropriate data management in such systems is challenging as demonstrated by the numerous current efforts [17]. Challenges come from several factors as the large scale, the evolutivity and dynamicity inherent to such systems: participant sites may disappear, appear, change and more generally system characteristic evolve. Ideally, the configuration of middleware running on such systems should also evolve so as to better fit the current system characteristics and user/application requirements.

This paper focuses on context-aware data management services in grids with the aim of constructing self-adaptive middleware. The contribution is twofold. First it proposes a framework to facilitate the development of context management services. The reason is that, even a context management service, is context specific [16]: the context management service depends on the deployment environment and the service using it. For example, context management required by an adaptable cache service differs from the one required by a data visualization service. So, being able to have an appropriate context management service is the first step to provide context-aware services. Second contribution concerns context-aware cache services. It is somehow an illustration of a new context-aware data management service. Our proposal allows the definition and self adaptation of logical networks of semantic cache services. Cache services are deployed across the grid. A context-aware cooperation among them is established and maintained to improve querying distributed data sources.

The paper is organized as follows. Section 2 introduces our cache services. They are our target application as they will use context services to become

A. Hameurlain (Ed.): Globe 2008, LNCS 5187, pp. 34–45, 2008.

context aware caches. Section 3 describes the context framework we propose. Section 4 presents context aware caching whereas section 5 reports experimental results. Section 6 presents a brief related work on caching and context architectures. Section 7 concludes the paper and introduces our future works.

2   Key Elements for Caching Service in Data Grids

Caching is crucial to optimize performances in data grids. This section briefly describes novel approaches we have proposed for semantic collaborative caching in large scale data querying systems.

2.1   Semantic Dual Caching in Grids

Dual cache [12] is designed to improve query evaluation over data sources distributed across a grid. It maximizes advantages of semantic caching which are the reduction of both data transfers and query computation. It clearly distinguishes these two goals by managing a couple composed of a query cache and an object cache. The query cache manages query results. An entry is identified by a query signature and the query answer is stored as the set of identifiers of the relevant objects. Objects themselves are in the related object cache, not in the query cache. The object cache has no obligation to synchronize its content with the query cache.

Such an approach is particularly relevant in grids, where large amounts of data are manipulated. In fact, in this context it may be impossible for caches to store objects associated to certain queries, whereas keeping in the cache the references to the objects avoids the re-evaluation of potentially costly, distributed queries. In addition, Ad-hoc tuning of both caches is possible to enhance global performances.

2.2   Cache Networks in Large Scale Environments

Load balancing is critical in large scale systems, where servers may become bottlenecks. Cooperative caching, using other caches during cache miss resolution, is relevant in such a context, in particular considering the concept of proximity function [10]. Proximity reflects the relevance of the cooperation between two caches. Proximity is context dependant. We propose *physic* and *semantic* proximities. Physic proximity measures the efficiency of data transfers. It enables to consider several parameters like bandwidth, latency or behaviors of hosts where caches are deployed (CPU, load, etc.). Semantic proximity is used to measure the similarity of queries processed by caches. It may be based, for example, on the type of data managed or on the interests their clients share.

Proximity based cooperation is particularly interesting using dual caches, which are composed of different caches. On the one hand semantic proximity for query caches helps avoiding processing queries already stored in other caches. On the other hand, physic proximity for object caches optimizes data transfers, using only caches providing an efficient data access.

2.3 Limits of Semantic Collaborative Caching in Variable Contexts

Considering a large scale system, the idea is to create logical networks of cooperating caches based on ad-hoc proximity functions. As shown [12], [10] cooperating dual-caches result in great improvement in performances in stable systems. However, to consider variable environments as usual in large scale systems, it is mandatory to extend this approaches to tackle dynamic reconfiguration. Our proposal is to introduce context-aware caching services, relying on the use of specific context managers. Each context-aware cache has its own context manager created by using the framework proposed in section 3.

3   Context Manager Framework

This section presents a Context Manager framework *CMF* which makes easier the development of context-aware services. It helps to define Context Managers for monitoring relevant elements from environment and notifying services about situations requiring an adaptation. Section 3.1 introduces the context manager framework and its application to a cache service. Section 3.2 details main concepts for modeling contexts. Section 3.3 describes the context evaluation process and section 3.4 gives an overview of architecture aspects.

3.1   Overview

By considering that each service has its own context and that a context management is context-aware itself [20], adding context management to many different services in a large infrastructure as a data grids is a challenge [17]. A context manager framework is a solution to deploy quickly reliable and efficient context-aware services in a grid. The management of context from a service comes down to the definition of what information (called contextual information) we are interested in surrounding the environment of this service, to the description of relevant states (called situations) of this environment and to choose the right reactions when situations occur.

CMF focuses on environment and situations modeling. A context manager does not apply direct adaptations but it provides enriched messages to an adaptation layer. The framework allows to define category of context management which can be instantiated by specific services. A graph approach is used to describe the schema of the environment to monitor and the set of relevant situations. A context manager is flexible and follows new requirements of a context-aware service by adaptating context management and relevant situations themselves.

We consider cooperative semantic caches as case study and running example. The objective is to introduce context-awareness so as to better cope with changes in the environement. We focus on the problem of updating logic networks of cooperating caches. Each cache uses its own context manager to choose locally an appropriated stragegy.

3.2   Context Modeling

CMF is based on two main concepts: *Environment* and *Situation*. Each of them uses a graph representation.

Definition 1. *An environment represents the set of information a context manager has to monitor. A workflow schema gives an enriched view of these contextual information. An environment is composed of measures, transformation links and sensors. Two types of measure exist: raw ones (from sensors) and calculated ones. Transformation links are aggregation or interpretation operations for defining adapted view on contextual data. A measure is defined by its type and its value. Sensors play the role of physical and software sensors.*

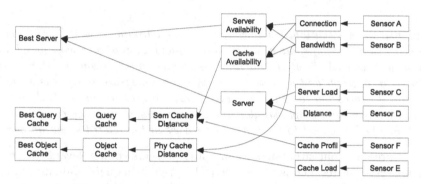

Fig. 1. Environment model of a cache service

Figure 1 presents a part of environment for a cache service. The graph should be read right to left. Measures to the right express consolidated data from various sensors: connection state and network bandwidth of resources (server or cache), server load, estimated distance of a resource, semantic profile information of cache and cache load. These types of measure obtain their values from sensors. server availability and cache availability are enhanced measures that aggregate data from bandwidth and connection measures. server is also a enhanced measure that aggregates server load and distance measures for defining a quality estimated of servers, best server measure that aggregates availability and quality measure of server to deduce the best servers, semantic cache distance built from cache profile and availability, physical cache distance built from cache load and bandwidth, query cache and object cache gives the proximity of a cache (close or not) using respective distance value, etc.

Figure 2 is an example of environment instantiation. It shows the environment for an object cache which uses many object measures. Related transformations are managed by a context manager. A set of sensors (instances of sensor type B) populates different bandwidth data (one sensor can populate several bandwidth data). A set of sensors (instances of sensor type E) populates Cache load value for each caches listed in the context manager. A couple of values (`bandwidth`, `cache load`) is aggregated to form a merged and enriched representation of `physical distance` for each cache. They are transformed in a binary value (`near, far`) in each `object cache` information (one per cache). Finally the `best object cache` measure has only one instance, its value is the list of caches considered as being `near`.

Fig. 2. Snapshot of an Environment Instantiation

Definition 2. *A situation is a subgraph of the environment workflow. It represents a relevant state of some measures and depicts a situation involving adaptations for a service. A situation is defined by a name, a set of constraint measures organized in a graph and a message. A constraint measure is a measure using a constraint expression to define a relevant state of the environment. Situations are represented with a graph, similar to environments. A message consists in information which are sent to the target service when the related situation occurs.*

Figure 3 presents four situations. Figure 3(a) presents some relevant situations involving server states. Let us supose server 1 is used by a query evaluated though the target cache. When server 1 becomes unavailable the situation 1 occurs and the cache service is alerted with the information of the best available server. When server 1 has a bad impact on quality of service (server load greater than 80%), the situation 2 occurs: the context manager send a message containing all usefull information for the cache service to update its cooperation strategy. Figure 3(b) focuses on cache states: the situation 3 occurs when all query caches cannot match with semantic proximity requirements, the situation 4 occurs when only object cache 1 is not near enough to the target cache service.

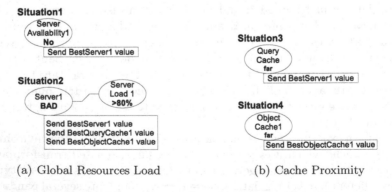

(a) Global Resources Load   (b) Cache Proximity

Fig. 3. Examples of Relevant Situations for caching

3.3 Context Evaluation

Definition 3. *Context evaluation is the process to monitor the environment and to identify relevant situations that occur. The result of an evaluation is a set of situations (at least one) which are sent to a target service with related messages.*

A set of situations is linked to an environment state. The evaluation of a situation consists in identifying measures in the environment which match with the situation constraints. This comparison process gives a quality matching for each measure in the situation. Each situation has a global probability value which is built by combining all quality matching. Interpretation and aggregation links are used to weight quality matching of situation measures. This weighting tags are relied on environnement and are implementing in environnement components as presented in Section 3.4.

The most important task for situation evaluation is quality matching of situation measures. Different measure types can have very different value types and each type of value requires a specific comparison process for evaluating matching between the value of an environnement measure and a constraint expression from a situation measure. The language to define constraint expressions is relied to measure type : simple comparison expression as $X>5$ and $X<10$ and semantic description as OWL schema, for example, require very different comparison process. It means comparison function for quality matching evaluation of situation measures is a generic concept which is instantiated specifically for each measure type. This relies to implementation of measure component as presented in Section 3.4.

Moreover the context evaluation process deals with the problem of situation filtering which comes from overlap situations and situation priorities. Situations are classified in a generalization/specialization tree to avoid evaluation of situations which subsume other ones. Only situations at leaf position are evaluated if these ones have good global evaluation value. Overlap situations are also filtered by their global evaluation value only.

3.4 CMF Architecture

CMF (see figure 4) accepts in input an environment schema and some initial and common situations and generates a set of context managers related to each input description.

Concepts are implemented as components of context manager services (see figure 4). An **Environment Manager** monitors an instantiated schema, provides

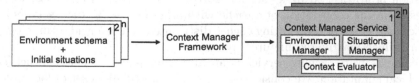

Fig. 4. Instantiation of several Context Managers

historical capabilities and takes into account resource and communication failures. A `Situations Manager` is a repository of situation to deal with. A `Context Evaluator` provides mechanism to identify situations which occur. Some tools are added as a `Communication Layer` which plays the role of an interface between the context manager and the outside to hide input data flow and a `Configuration Layer` which receives configuration commands from different services to adapt the context manager to new requirements of target service and infrastructure.

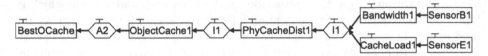

Fig. 5. Snapshot of a context workflow representation

The environment schema defined in the `Environment Manager`, as shown in figure 5, is the composition of components of different types using Fractal model [7]: A measure provides features to store contextual information and is defined by a type, a name, a value, a status (enable, disable, outdated) and a comparison function. This function is used by the context evaluation process to identify measures that match with situations. `Sensors` form an abstraction layer and communicate with real sensors which are shared with all context managers. An `Aggregator` transforms several measure values into a new enriched value by aggregation of input values. In figure 5, `A1` aggregates values of components `Bandwidth1` and `CacheLoad1` and stores the result value in `PhyCacheDist1`. An `Interpretor` transforms one measure value and adapts its representation. In figure 5 interpretor `I1` transforms the `PhyCacheDist1` value (numerical data) into a binary value (nearest or not) in `ObjectCache1`.

4   Context-Aware Caching

This section presents reconfiguration opportunities for a cache service and the architecture of a context-aware caching service. A scenario shows the dynamic reconfiguration of a virtual cache networks using local cache reconfigurations.

Reconfiguration opportunities. Several adaptations of a cache service may be worth depending on the evolution of the context. Dynamic reconfiguration may impact all aspects of a cache. Such adaptations may be simple local tuning actions as allocated memory growing or replacement protocol update. Some operations can have a larger impact on the environnement as adaptation of the resolution protocol used by a cache to solve cache misses. In this case, we are interested in the cooperation of a cache with other entities as data servers and other caches. A set of cooperating caches distributed across a grid form a logical network which may be reconfigured dynamically.

A context-aware caching service is an autonomous cache service which can apply local adaptation. We consider the following postulate: a set of local adaptations increase or keep constant the global performance. Figure 6 illustrates the global architecture of a context-aware cache. It is based on an adaptable cache service, associated to a specific `Context Manager` (instantiated with CMF), according to the needs of the considered cache service, and an `Adaptation Manager`. We consider the cache service is built with ACS [11]. To ease adaptation ACS decomposes a cache service according to the separation of concerns principle using components. In particular, the `Resolution Manager` implements the protocol used to retrieve a missing object. The `Context Manager` component produces high level events to be considered by the `Adaptation Manager`.

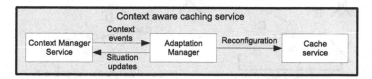

Fig. 6. Context-Aware Cache Service

The `Adaptation Manager` is the "decisional element" which gets events from the `Context Manager` and initiates the adaptation of the cache service. Reconfiguration may correspond to parameterization (to change servers or sibling caches involved when a cache miss occurs) or composition (adding, removing or replacing components as a query analyzer and evaluator in case of server's failure to enhance availability). In this application, the `Adaptation Manager` is based on ECA rules. It has to be noted that the `Adaptation Manager` is also in charge of the execution model. It defines if the coupling between the event and reconfiguration phases is immediate or delayed. It also introduces execution plans, if several events/reconfigurations have to be considered at a same time (using random, sequential, parallel or hybrid strategies).

An example of updating a cooperation topology of caches. Figure 7 shows the sequence of reconfiguration state from a reliable cache networks to another one after some server shutdowns. In state **A** (Figure 7.a) the Context-Aware Caching Service 1 (CAC1) uses server S1 to retrieve missing objects. Its context is built from knowledge acquired from Server S1&S2, CAC2&3. When Server S1 shuts down (due to a server load or some physical network link problems) the context in CAC1 changes and the `Adaptation Manager` chooses a new strategy to resolve missing objects. The state **B** (Figure 7.b) represents this situation, the server S2 cooperates now with CAC1. The state **C** (Figure 7.c) shows the results of the server S2 unavailability. The context of CAC1 changes again and some cooperation links are established with CAC2 and CAC3 to define a new logical cache network. The state **D** (Figure 7.d) illustrates the consequence of a change in CAC3 context. A new cooperation link is established between CAC3 and server S3. CAC2 does not use directly server S3 because it does not appear in its context. In general case a service has a partial view of its environment. The state **E** (Figure 7.e) is an example of stable situation where CAC1 has stopped its cooperation with CAC2.

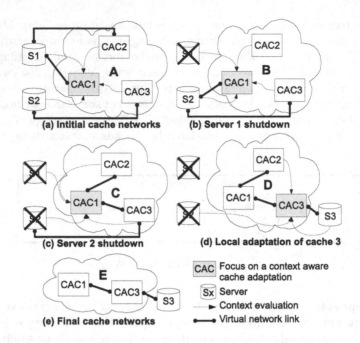

Fig. 7. An example of updating a cooperation topology of caches

5   Experimentations

The main objective of the experiments presented bellow is to evaluate the impact of dynamic reconfiguration of caches, according to load on data sources and caches, in large scale data querying. Three scenarios are studied. (1) The first one considers data querying where a cache directly resolves a cache miss using servers. (2) The second one considers dynamic reconfiguration, adapting direct resolution via servers to a cooperative caching approach (using semantic proximity for the query cache and physic proximity for the object cache). (3) The last one considers a first reconfiguration, enabling to adapt a direct resolution via servers to cooperative caching, and a second reconfiguration, to change cooperative caching into a direct resolution using local duplicated servers.

Experiments have been done using Swiss-Prot [2], a biological database of protein sequences and Gedeon middleware, providing a direct access to a sequence its identifier and query evaluation capabilities. For our experiments, we have used the French grid platform Grid5000. Clusters at four sites (Lille, Nancy, Rennes and Toulouse) have been used. Technical behaviors of the different sites and networks can be found in the Grid5000 website (http://www.grid5000.fr/). Swiss-Prot has been horizontally partitioned in three equally sized files, managed by one node, in order to parallelize evaluations. Original servers use nodes on Nancy, Rennes and Toulouse, whereas duplicated servers are based on three nodes at Toulouse. Ten clients (two at Lille, two at Rennes, three at Nancy and three at Toulouse) with their own 325Mb dual cache (10Mb for the query cache and 315Mb for the object cache) generates queries, according to our own workload generator (considering specific behaviors, like semantic locality or specific interests). Details on the workload generation can be found in [10]. Measures and dynamic adaptation(s) only concern the cache of one particular client (deployed at Toulouse). All other caches always directly resolve a cache miss via the original servers.

Mean response times obtained for the different scenarios clearly show the benefits or dynamic reconfiguration for such a context. Mean response time decreases when dynamic reconfiguration(s) is/are considered: 34.6 seconds without reconfiguration, 28 seconds considering cooperative caching adaptation and 12,3 seconds considering both cooperative caching and duplication reconfigurations.

6   Related Work

This paper tackles different domains related to data grid management. In this section we present some of the main works related to context, grid caching and cache frameworks.

Software adaptation is not a brand new problem, however the needs of good tuned services in new large and complex environment put this issue in front. The term of context has been rediscovered [18], [9] but without a clear definition nor a consensus. Both context model families exist [5]: user centered model with its physical environment, which allows to develop context-aware middleware [3], and system centered model which gives resource-aware middleware [7] using properties with dynamic values. CMF is at the intersection of these both families and has to answer to large scale and performance issues related to the grid environment. Existing context toolkits are based on a static and centralized approach as [8] or provides limited and not proved scaling approach as [6]. Monitoring middleware on grids exist too, as [19] that proposes a complete solution to monitor, react and manage the grid. CMF is a lighter solution for service adaptation and not a global grid management.

Mediation like approach are common in grid caching. Intelligent Cache Management [1] focuses on the problem of network latency and proposes to store data in distributed DB replicated across the grid. A distributed cache service is proposed in [4], that offers semantic cache functionalities by using hierarchical cache architecture and a global catalogue. Some proposals focus on load balancing and fault tolerance in large scale environments, like dCache [13] for data management in particles physics. Dual cache is orthogonal to these works.

Many cache frameworks permit the construction of static caches and well adapted to specific cache strategies. The most relevant frameworks for large scale data management are certainly CaLi [21], for its cooperative cache features, and Perseus [14] for its dynamic adaptation capabilities. [15] presents the properties of an adaptative framework for the grid. ACS enables semantic caching and considers interaction with a `Context Manager` to supply capabilities for autonomous dynamic reconfigurations.

7   Conclusion and Future Works

In this paper we have presented a context-aware grid caching approach based on the combination of a context manager framework and a cache service framework. The context manager framework provides environment and situations description model to enhance the definition of well-adapted context managers. The cache service framework allows us to define semantic cache services with adaptation capabilities. A rule based execution model uses information from the Context Manager to choose the right adaptation strategies. This paper does not tackle the problem of context initialisation and context adaptation, however the context architecture allows dynamic adaptation and we work on an infrastructure that supports the definition of autonomous context managers. The cost of information monitoring and adaptation is important for context-aware services in a grid environment, futhermore we work on the definition of a cost model at the context level so us to better understand the impact of monitoring.

References

1. Ahmed, M.U., Zaheer, R.A., Qadir, M.A.: Intelligent cache management for data grid. In: Australian WS on Grid computing and e-research, pp. 5–12 (2005)
2. Boeckmann, B., Bairoch, A., Apweiler, R., Blatter, M.-C., Estreicher, A., Gasteiger, E., Martin, M.J., Michoud, K., O'Donovan, C., Phan, I., Pilbout, S., Schneider, M.: The swiss-prot protein knowledgebase and its supplement trembl in 2003. Nucleic Acids Res. 31(1), 365–370 (2003)
3. Capra, L., Emmerich, W., Mascolo, C.: Carisma: Context-aware reflective middleware system for mobile applications. IEEE Transactions on Software Engineering 29(10), 929–945 (2003)
4. Cardenas, Y., Pierson, J.-M., Brunie, L.: Uniform distributed cache service for grid computing. In: Intl WS on Database and Expert Systems Applications, pp. 351–355 (2005)
5. Cheung-Foo-Wo, D., Tigli, J.-Y., Lavirotte, S., Riveill, M.: Self-adaptation of event-driven component-oriented middleware using aspects of assembly. Intl WS on Middleware for Pervasive and Ad-Hoc Computing (2007)
6. Coutaz, J., Rey, G.: Foundation for a theory of contextors. In: CADUI 2002, pp. 283–302. ACM Publication, New York (2002)
7. David, P.-C., Ledoux, T.: An aspect-oriented approach for developing self-adaptive fractal components. In: Intl. Symp. on Software Composition (2006)
8. Dey, A., Salber, D., Abowd, G.: A conceptual framework and a toolkit for supporting the rapid prototyping of context-aware applications. Special issue on Context-Aware Computing, in the Human-Computer Interaction 16 (2001)
9. Dey, A.K., Salber, M., Futakawa, D.a., Abowd, G.D.: An architecture to support context-aware applications. GVU Technical Report GIT-GVU-99-23 (1999)
10. d'Orazio, L., Jouanot, F., Denneulin, Y., Labbé, C., Roncancio, C., Valentin, O.: Distributed semantic caching in grid middleware. In: Wagner, R., Revell, N., Pernul, G. (eds.) DEXA 2007. LNCS, vol. 4653. Springer, Heidelberg (2007)
11. d'Orazio, L., Jouanot, F., Labbé, C., Roncancio, C.: Building adaptable cache services. In: Intl WS on Middleware for Grid Computing, November 2005, pp. 1–6 (2005)

12. d'Orazio, L., Labbé, C., Roncancio, C., Jouanot, F.: Query and data caching in grid middleware. In: Conf. latinoamericana de computacion de alto rendimiento (2007)
13. Fuhrmann, P., Gulzow, V.: Dcache, storage system for the future. In: European Conf. on Parallel and Distributed Computing, pp. 1106–1113 (2006)
14. Garcia-Banuelos, L., Duong, P.-Q., Collet, C.: A Component based Infrastructure for Customized Persistent Object Management. In: Intl WS on Parallel and Distributed Databases: innovative applications and new architectures, Prague, Czech Republic (2003)
15. Gounaris, A., Paton, N.W., Sakellariou, R., Fernandes, A.A.A.: Adaptive query processing and the grid: Opportunities and challenges. In: DEXA Workshops, pp. 506–510. IEEE Computer Society, Los Alamitos (2004)
16. Kintzig, C., Poulain, G., Privat, G., Favennec, P.-N. (eds.): Making context explicit in communicating objects. Communicating with Smart (2003)
17. Pierson, J., Brunie, L.: Special issue on data management in grids. Concurrency and Computation: Practice and Experience 19(16), 2105–2107 (2001)
18. Schilit, B., Adams, N., Want, R.: Context-aware computing applications. In: IEEE WS on Mobile Computing Systems and Applications, pp. 85–90 (1994)
19. Truong, H.-L., Fahringer, T.: Self-managing sensor-based middleware for performance monitoring and data integration in grids. In: Intl. Parallel and Distributed Processing Symp. (2005)
20. Winograd, G.: Architectures for context. Human Computer Interaction 16, 409–419 (2001)
21. Zola, J.: Cali, efficient library for cache implementation. In: Mexican Intl Conf. on Computer Science, pp. 415–420 (2004)

Query Propagation in a P2P Data Integration System in the Presence of Schema Constraints

Tadeusz Pankowski[1,2]

[1] Institute of Control and Information Engineering,
Poznań University of Technology, Poland
[2] Faculty of Mathematics and Computer Science,
Adam Mickiewicz University, Poznań, Poland
tadeusz.pankowski@put.poznan.pl

Abstract. This paper addresses the problem of data integration in a P2P environment, where each peer stores schema of its local data, mappings between the schemas, and some schema constraints. The goal of the integration is to answer queries formulated against a chosen peer. The answer consists of data stored in the queried peer as well as data of its direct and indirect partners. We focus on defining and using mappings, schema constraints, query propagation across the P2P system, and query reformulation in such scenario. The main focus is the exploitation of constraints for merging results from different peers to derive more complex information, and utilizing constraint knowledge to query propagation and the merging strategy. We show how the discussed method has been implemented in SixP2P system.

1 Introduction

In a peer-to-peer (P2P) data integration scenario, the user issues queries against an arbitrarily chosen peer and expects that the answer will include relevant data stored in all P2P connected data sources. The data sources are related by means of schema mappings. A query must be propagated to all peers in the system along semantic paths of mappings and reformulated accordingly. The partial answers must be merged and sent back to the user peer [9,14,16].

Much work has been done on data integration systems both with a mediated (global) schema and in P2P architecture, where the schema of any peer can play the role of the mediated schema [4,9,10,19]. There is also a number of systems built in P2P data integration paradigm [8], notably Piazza [17], PeerDB [12]). In these research the focus was on overcoming syntactic heterogeneity and schema mappings were used to specify how data structured under one schema (the source schema) can be transformed into data structured under another schema (the target schema) [6,7]. A little work has been paid on how schema constraints influence the query propagation.

In this paper we discuss the problem of query propagation where schemas are defined by means of tree-pattern formulas and there are constraints (XML

A. Hameurlain (Ed.): Globe 2008, LNCS 5187, pp. 46–57, 2008.
© Springer-Verlag Berlin Heidelberg 2008

functional dependencies) defined over the schemas. We show how mutual relationships between schema constraints and queries can influence both propagation of queries and merging of answers. Taking into account such interrelationships may improve both efficiency of the system and information content included in answers. We shortly show how the issues under consideration have been implemented SixP2P (*Semantic Integration of XML in P2P environment*) system.

In Section 1, formal concepts underlying XML data integration are discussed. The main theoretical result concerning query propagation and merging of answers is included in Section 3. In Sections 4 we show some details about query propagation in SixP2P implementation. Section 5 concludes the paper.

2   Pattern-Based Schemas, Mappings and Queries

2.1   Schemas

In this paper an *XML schema* (a *schema* for short) will be understood as a *tree-pattern formula* [4,14]. Schemas will be used to specify structures of *XML trees*. Other properties of XML trees are defined as *schema constraints*.

Definition 1. *A schema over a set L of labels and a set* **x** *of variables is an expression conforming to the syntax:*

$$
\begin{aligned}
S &::= /l[E] \\
E &::= l = x \mid l[E] \mid E \wedge ... \wedge E,
\end{aligned}
\tag{1}
$$

where $l \in L$, *and* x *is a variable in* **x**. *If variable names are significant, we will write* $S(\mathbf{x})$.

Example 1. The schema S_1 in Figure 1 can be specified as follows:

$$
S_1(x_1, x_2, x_3, x_4) := /pubs[pub[title = x_1 \wedge year = x_2 \wedge \\
author[name = x_3 \wedge university = x_4]]]
$$

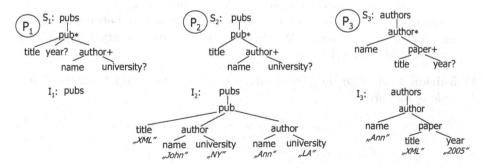

Fig. 1. XML schema trees S_1, S_2, S_3, and their instances I_1, I_2 and I_3, located in peers P_1, P_2, and P_3, respectively

Definition 2. *Let S be a schema over $\mathbf{x}$ and let an atom $l = x$ occur in S. Then the path P starting in the root and ending in l is called the type of the variable x, denoted $type_S(x) = P$.*

Example 2. The type of x_1 in schema S_1 is
$$type_{S_1}(x_1) = /pubs/pub/title.$$

An XML database consists of a set of XML data trees. It will be useful to represent an XML tree I with schema $S(\mathbf{x})$ as a pair $(S(\mathbf{x}), \Omega)$, where Ω is a set of valuations of variables in $\mathbf{x}$.

Definition 3. *Let $Str \cup \{\perp\}$ be a set of strings used as values of text nodes, where $\perp$ is the distinguished null value. Let $\mathbf{x}$ be a set of variable names. A valuation ω for variables in $\mathbf{x}$ is a function*

$$\omega : \mathbf{x} \to Str \cup \{\perp\},$$

assigning values in $Str \cup \{\perp\}$ to variables in $\mathbf{x}$.

Each instance of a schema S can be represented by a pair (S, Ω), where Ω is a set of valuations for variables occurring in S. However, this representation is not unique, since elements in instance trees can be grouped and nested in different ways. By a *canonical instance* we will understand the instance with the maximal width, i.e. the instance where subtrees corresponding to valuations are pair-wise disjoint. For example, the instance I_2 in Figure 1 is not canonical since two authors are nested under one publication. In SixP2P we use canonical instances to handle XML trees efficiently – in particular to merge XML trees with discovering missing values.

2.2 Schema Mappings

The key issue in data integration is this of *schema mapping*. Schema mapping is a specification defining how data structured under one schema (the *source schema*) is to be transformed into data structured under another schema (the *target schema*). In the theory of relational data exchange, *source-to-target dependencies* (STDs) [2] are usually used to express schema mappings [6].

A schema mapping specifies the semantic relationship between a source schema and a target schema. We define it as a source-to-target dependency adapted for XML data [4,15].

Definition 4. *A mapping from a source schema S to a target schema T is a formula of the form*

$$m_{S \to T} := \forall \mathbf{x}(S(\mathbf{x}) \Rightarrow \exists \mathbf{y} T(\mathbf{x}', \mathbf{y})), \tag{2}$$

where $\mathbf{x}' \subseteq \mathbf{x}$, and $\mathbf{y} \cap \mathbf{x} = \emptyset$.

The result of a mapping is the canonical instance of the right-hand side schema, where each variables $y \in \mathbf{y}$ has the $\perp$ (*null*) value.

Example 3. The mapping m_{31} from S_3 to S_1 is specified as:

$$m_{31} := \forall x_1, x_2, x_3(S_3(x_1, x_2, x_3) \Rightarrow \exists x_4 S_1(x_2, x_3, x_1, x_4)).$$

Then, for $I_3 = (S_3(x_1, x_2, x_3), \Omega)$, where $\Omega = \{(Ann, XML, 2005)\})$,

$$m_{31}(I_3) = J,$$

where $J = (S_1(x_1, x_2, x_3, x_4), \{(XML, 2005, Ann, \bot)\})$.

The set $\Omega' = \{(XML, 2005, Ann, \bot)\}$ is created from Ω using variable correspondences specified in the mapping m_{31}.

2.3   Queries and Query Reformulation

Given a schema S, a *qualifier* ϕ over S is a formula built from constants, as well as paths and variables occurring in S. Let $m_{S \to T} = \forall \mathbf{x}(S(\mathbf{x}) \Rightarrow \exists \mathbf{y} T(\mathbf{x}', \mathbf{y}))$ be a mapping from a source schema S to a target schema T and ϕ be a *query qualifier* over S. A query q over the mapping $m_{S \to T}$ with qualifier ϕ is

$$q := \forall \mathbf{x}(S(\mathbf{x}) \wedge \phi(\mathbf{x}) \Rightarrow \exists \mathbf{y} T(\mathbf{x}', \mathbf{y})). \tag{3}$$

For short, we will denote a query as $q = (m_{S \to T}, \phi)$.

Let $q = (m_{S \to T}, \phi)$ be a query from S to T and $I = (S, \Omega)$ be an instance of S. An answer to a query $q(I)$ is such an instance $J = (T, \Omega)$ of T that its description Ω' is defined as:

$$\Omega' = \{\omega.restrict(\mathbf{x}') \cup null(\mathbf{y}) \mid \omega \in \Omega \wedge \phi(\omega) = true\}, \tag{4}$$

where $\omega.restrict(\mathbf{x}')$ is the restriction of the valuation ω to the variables in $\mathbf{x}'$, and $null(\mathbf{y})$ is a valuation assigning nulls to all variables in $\mathbf{y}$.

Example 4. The query

$$q_{12} = (m_{S_1(x_1, x_2, x_3, x_4) \to S_2(x_1, x_3, x_4)}, x_3 = \text{``John''} \wedge x_2 = \text{``2005''}),$$

filters an instance of the source schema S_1 according to the qualifier and produces an instance of the schema S_2.

A query is issued by the user against a peer. The user sees the target schema $T(\mathbf{z})$, and defines a qualifier $\phi(\mathbf{z})$, so initially the query is of the form $q = (m_{T(\mathbf{z}) \to T(\mathbf{z})}, \phi(\mathbf{z}))$. When the query is propagated to a source peer with the schema $S(\mathbf{x})$, it must be reformulated accordingly. Thus, the query is to be reformulated into a query $q' = (m_{S(\mathbf{x}) \to T(\mathbf{x}', \mathbf{y})}, \phi'(\mathbf{x}))$.

The reformulation is performed as follows (Figure 2):

1. We want to determine the qualifier $\phi'(\mathbf{x})$ over the source schema $S(\mathbf{x})$. To do this we use the mapping $m_{S(\mathbf{x}) \to T(\mathbf{x}', \mathbf{y})}$.
2. The qualifier $\phi'(\mathbf{x})$ is obtained as the result of rewriting the qualifier $\phi(\mathbf{z})$

$$\phi'(\mathbf{x}) := \phi(\mathbf{z}).rewrite(T(\mathbf{z}), T(\mathbf{x}', \mathbf{y})). \tag{5}$$

The rewriting consists in appropriate replacement of variable names. A variable $z \in \mathbf{z}$ occurring in $\phi(\mathbf{z})$ is replaced by such a variable $x \in \mathbf{x}'$ that the type of z in $T(\mathbf{z})$ is equal to the type of x in $T(\mathbf{x}', \mathbf{y})$. If such $x \in \mathbf{x}'$ does not exist, the query is not rewritable.

$$S(x) \xrightarrow{\; S(x) \Rightarrow \exists y\, T(x',y) \;} T(z)$$

$$\varphi'(x)\qquad\qquad\qquad\qquad\qquad\qquad \varphi(z)$$

$$\varphi'(x):= \varphi(z).rewrite(T(z),T(x',y)),$$
for each $z \in$ **z**, replace: $z \to x$, such that
$x \in$ **x'** and $type_{T(z)}(z) = type_{T(x',y)}(x)$

Fig. 2. Reformulation of a query $(m_{T(\mathbf{z}) \to T(\mathbf{z})}, \phi(\mathbf{z}))$ into a query $(m_{S(\mathbf{x}) \to T(\mathbf{x'},\mathbf{y})}, \phi'(\mathbf{x}))$ using the mapping $\forall \mathbf{x}(S(\mathbf{x}) \Rightarrow \exists \mathbf{y} T(\mathbf{x'}, \mathbf{y}))$

Example 5. For the query $q_{11} = (m_{S_1(x_1,x_2,x_3,x_4) \to S_1(x_1,x_2,x_3,x_4)}, x_3 = \text{``}John\text{''})$, we have the following reformulation for its propagation to S_2,

$$q_{21} = (m_{S_2(x_1,x_2,x_3) \to S_1(x_1,x_4,x_2,x_3)}, x_2 = \text{``}John\text{''}),$$

since $type_{S_1(x_1,x_2,x_3,x_4)}(x_3) = type_{S_1(x_1,x_4,x_2,x_3)}(x_2) = /pubs/pub/author/name$.

3   Deciding about Merging and Propagation Modes

In this section we will discuss haw the existence of *XML functional dependencies* (*XFDs*) defined over schemas can influence the way of propagating queries and merging partial answers. Our aim is the exploitation of functional dependencies for increasing the amount of information obtained in the process of merging partial results. While merging data from different sources, we can use *XFDs* to discover some *missing values*, i.e. values denoted by $\perp$.

Definition 5. *An XML functional dependency (XFD) over a set L of labels and a set* **x** *of variables is an expression with the syntax:*

$$
\begin{aligned}
f &::= /P[C]/.../P[C], \\
P &::= l \mid P/l, \\
C &::= TRUE \mid P = x \mid C \wedge ... \wedge C,
\end{aligned}
\tag{6}
$$

where $l \in L$, and x is a variable in **x**. *If variable names are significant, we will write $f(\mathbf{x})$.*

Example 6. XFD over S_3 is

$$f(x_2) := /authors/author/paper[title = x_2]/year,$$

meaning that the value of $f(x_2)$ is uniquely determined by the values of x_2.

Types of variables are defined in the same way as for schemas. Let

$$f = /P_1[C_1]/.../P_i[\cdots \wedge P_{ij} = x_j \wedge \cdots]/.../P_n[C_n],$$

be an XFD. Then: $type_f(x_j) = /P_1/.../P_i/P_{ij}$, additionally, $type(f) = /P_1/.../P_n$.

An XFD $f(\mathbf{x})$ says that the value $[\![f(\mathbf{x})(\omega)]\!]$ of $f(\mathbf{x})$ according to the XPath semantics [18], is uniquely determined by a valuation ω of variables in **x**

Let $f(x_1, ..., x_k)$ be an XFD over $S(\mathbf{x})$, and x be a variable in **x** such that $type_S(x) = type(f)$. An XML tree $I = (S(\mathbf{x}), \Omega)$ satisfies this XFD, if for any two valuations $\omega, \omega' \in \Omega$, the implication holds:

$$\omega(x_1, ..., x_k) = \omega'(x_1, ..., x_k) \Rightarrow \omega(x) = \omega'(x),$$

i.e. equality of arguments implies the equality of values.

Thus, XFD can be used to infer missing value of the variable x in the data tree that is expected to satisfy this XFD [14]. Let ω and ω' be two valuations for variables in $\mathbf{x}$ and:

$$\begin{aligned}\omega(x_1, ..., x_k) &= \omega'(x_1, ..., x_k), \\ \omega(x) &\neq \perp, \text{ and } \omega'(x) = \perp.\end{aligned} \tag{7}$$

Then, we can take $\omega'(x) := \omega(x)$.

Answers to a query propagated across the P2P systems must be collected and merged. In the merge operation we incorporate the discovery of missing values, i.e. null values $\perp$ are replaced everywhere where it is possible, and this replacement is based on XFD constraints.

Thus, it is important to decide which of the following two merging modes should be selected in the peer while partial answers are to be merged:

- *Partial merge* – A partial answer $q(I_S)$ obtained from the propagation is merged with the local answer $q(I_T)$ over the target schema. The answer is: $Ans_{part} = merge(q(I_S), q(I_T))$.
- *Full merge* – The whole instance I_T in the target peer is merged with received partial answer $q(I_S)$, and then the query is evaluated on the result of the merge. Then the answer is: $Ans_{full} = q(merge(q(I_S), I_T))$.

It is quite obvious that the full merge is much more costly than the partial one. However, during full merge more missing values can be discovered. Thus, it should be performed when there is a chance to discover missing values. The following Proposition 1 states the sufficient condition when there is no sense in applying full merge because no missing value can be discovered.

Proposition 1. *Let $S(\mathbf{x})$ be a schema, $f(\mathbf{z})$ be an XFD over $S(\mathbf{x})$, and $type(f) = type_S(x)$ for some $x \in \mathbf{x}$. Let q be a query with qualifier $\phi(\mathbf{y})$, $\mathbf{y} \subseteq \mathbf{x}$, I be the instance of S and I_A an answer to q received from a propagation. Then*

$$q(merge(I_A, I)) = merge(q(I), q(I_A)). \tag{8}$$

holds if one of the following two conditions holds

(a) $x \in \mathbf{y}$, or
(b) $\mathbf{z} \subseteq \mathbf{y}$.

Proof. The equality (8) does not hold if there are valuations $\omega' \in \Omega_{I_A}$ and $\omega \in \Omega_I$ such that $\omega'(x) = \perp$, $\omega(x) \neq \perp$, and $\omega'(\mathbf{z}) = \omega(\mathbf{z})$ (see (7)).

Let us consider conditions (a) and (b):

1. *Condition (a).* If $x \in \mathbf{y}$, then there cannot be $\omega' \in \Omega_{I_A}$ such that $\omega'(x) = \perp$, because then $\phi(\mathbf{y})(\omega') \neq true$. Thus, the theorem holds.
2. *Condition (b).* Let $\mathbf{z} \subseteq \mathbf{y}$. If there is such $\omega' \in \Omega_{I_A}$ that $\omega'(x) = \perp$, then:
   - if $\phi(\mathbf{y})(\omega') = true$ then $\omega' \in \Omega_{q(I)}$ and (8) holds;
   - if $\phi(\mathbf{y})(\omega') \neq true$ then ω can belong neither to $\Omega_{q(I)}$ nor to $\Omega_{q(I_A)}$, and ω is not relevant for discovering missing values. So, (8) holds.

To illustrate application of the above proposition let us consider a query about *John*'s data in peers P_2 and P_3 in Figure 1.

1. Let q be a query with qualifier $\phi_2 := x_2 = $ "*John*" in the peer P_2. There is also XFD $f_2 := /pubs/pub/author[name = x_2]/university$ specified over $S_2(x_1, x_2, x_3)$. In force of Proposition 1 there is no chance to discover any missing value of *John*'s university. Indeed, if we obtain an answer with $university = \bot$, then the real value is either in the local answer $q(I_2)$ or it does not occur in I_2 at all. So, in P_2 the partial merge should be performed. Performing the full join in this case is pointless.
2. Let q be a query with qualifier $\phi_3 := x_1 = $ "*John*" issued against peer P_3. There is XFD $f_3 := /authors/author/paper[title = x_2]/year$ specified over $S_3(x_1, x_2, x_3)$. Assumptions of Proposition 1 are not satisfied, so there is a chance to discover missing values of *year* using the full merge. Indeed, from P_2 we obtain the answer $q(I_2) = (S_3, \{(\text{"}John\text{"}, \text{"}XML\text{"}, \bot)\})$. The local answer $q(I_3)$ is empty. But performing the full merge and using f_3, we obtain: $q(merge((S_3, \{(\text{"}John\text{"}, \text{"}XML\text{"}, \bot)\}), (S_3, \{(\text{"}Ann\text{"}, \text{"}XML\text{"}, \text{"}2005\text{"})\}))) = (S_3, \{(\text{"}John\text{"}, \text{"}XML\text{"}, \text{"}2005\text{"})\})$. Thus, the year of *John*'s publication has been discovered and the using of full merge is justified.

The consequences of Proposition 1 impacts also the way of query propagations. The $P2P$ propagation (i.e. to all partners with the $P2P$ propagation mode) may be rejected because of avoiding cycles. However, when the analysis of the query qualifier and XFD's shows that there is a chance to discover missing values, the peer can decide to propagate the query with the *local* mode (i.e. it expects only the local answer from a partner, without further propagations). Such behavior can take place in peer P_3 in the case (2) discussed above.

4   Data Integration in SixP2P

4.1   Overall Architecture

SixP2P is built around a set of peers having a common architecture and communicating each other by sending (propagating) queries and returning answers. According to the P2P technology, there is not any central control over peer's behavior and each peer is autonomous in performing its operations, such as accepting queries, query answering and query propagation. Overall architecture of the system is depicted in Figure 3.

Each peer in SixP2P has its own local database consisting of two parts: data repository of data available to other peers, and 6P2P repository of data necessary for performing integration processes (e.g., information about partners, schemas, constraints, mappings, answers). Using the query interface (QI) a user formulates a query. The query execution module (QE) controls the process of query reformulation, query propagation to partners, merging of partial answers, discovering missing values, and returning partial answers [5,13,14,15]. Communication between peers (QAP) is realized by means of Web Services technology.

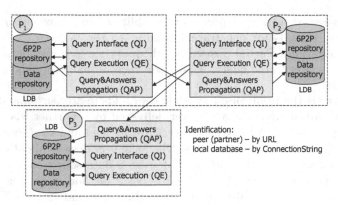

Fig. 3. Overall architecture of SixP2P

4.2 SixP2P Modeling Concepts

Basic notions constituting the SixP2P data model are: peers, data sources, schemas, constraints, mappings, queries, answers, and propagations.

1. A *peer*, @p, is identified by its URL address identifying also the Web Service representing the peer. There are two methods exported by a peer: *sendAnswer* – used by peers to send to @p the answer to a query received from @p, and *propagateQuery* – used by peers to send to @p a query to be answered (possibly with further propagations).
2. A *data source* is an XML document or an XML view over a centralized or distributed data. Different techniques can be used to implement such a view – it can be AXML documents [1,11], a gateway to another SixP2P system or even to different data integration systems. Thus, a community of various collaborating information integration engines can be created.
3. A *schema* is used to specify structural properties of the data source and also the structure of the intermediate answers to queries. In SixP2P, schemas are defined as tree-pattern formulas discussed in previous sections.
4. *Constraints* delivers additional knowledge about data. Two kinds of constraints are taken into consideration: *XML functional dependencies* (XFD) and XML *keys* [3,15]. XFD will be used to control query propagation and answer merging (especially to discover some *missing data*), and keys for eliminating duplicates and appropriate nesting of elements. In this paper we restrict ourselves to XFDs.
5. *Mappings* specify how data structured under a source schema is to be transformed into data conforming to a target schema [6,14]. Information provided by mappings is also used to query reformulation. In [14] we presented algorithms translating high level specifications of mappings, queries and constraints into XQuery programs.

6. A *query* issued against a peer can be split up to many *query threads* – one query threads for one trace incoming to the peer (corresponding to one propagation). Partial answers to all query threads are merged to produce the answer to the query. A peer can receive many threads of the same query.

7. An *answer* is the result of query evaluation. There are *partial* and *final* answers. A partial answer is an answer delivered by a partner who the query was propagated to. All partial answers are merged and transformed to obtain the final answer. In some cases (when the peer decides about discovering missing values, see Section 3), a whole peer's data source may be involved into the merging process. In [13] we discuss a method of dealing with *hard* inconsistent data, i.e. data that is other than null and violates XFDs. The method is based on trustworthiness of data sources.

8. A *propagation* is a relationship between a peer (the *target peer*) and another peer (the *source peer*) where the query has been sent (propagated) to. While propagating queries, the following three objectives are taken into account: (1) avoiding cycles, (2) deciding about propagation modes (*P2P* or *local*), and (3) deciding about merging modes (*full* or *partial*) (see Proposition 1).

4.3 SixP2P Database

A peer's database (PDB) consists of five tables: *Peer*, *Constraints*, *Partners* (Figure 4), *Queries*, and *Propagations* (Figure 5).

- *Peer*(*myPeer, myPatt, myData, xfdXQuery, keyXQuery*)–has exactly one row, where: *myPeer* – the URL of the peer owning the database; *myPatt* – the schema (tree-pattern formula) of the data source; *myData* – the peer's data source, i.e. an XML documents or an XML view over some data repositories. *xfdXQuery* and *keyXQuery* are XQuery programs obtained by the translation of constrain specifications, XFDs and keys, respectively [14].
- *Constraints*(*constrId, constrType, constrExp*) – stores information about the local data constraints (in this paper we discuss only XFDs).
- *Partners*(*partPeer, partPatt, mapXQuery*) – stores information about all peer's partners (acquaintances), where: *partPeer* – the URL of the partner; *partPatt* – the right-hand side of the schema mapping to the partner (variable names reflect correspondences between paths in the source and in the

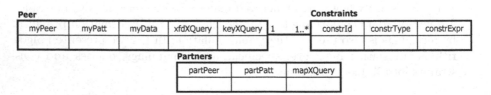

Fig. 4. Structure of tables *Peer*, *Constraints* and *Partners*

target schema). $mapXQuery$ is an XQuery program obtained by translation of the mapping determined by the $Peer.myPatt$ and $Partners.partPatt$[14].

- $Queries$ and $Propagations$ (Figure 5) maintain information about queries, $qryId$, and their threads, $qryThreadId$, managed in the SixP2P system. The user specifies a qualifier of the query, $myQualif$, as well as propagation ($propagMode$) and merging ($mergeMode$) modes.

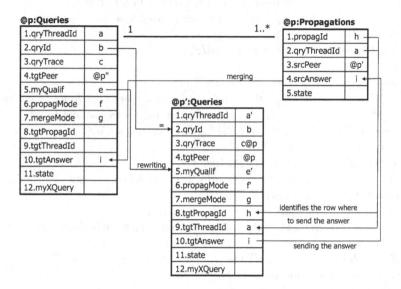

Fig. 5. $Queries$ and $Propagations$ tables in SixP2P. Sample data illustrates instances of tables when a query is propagated from a peer @p to a peer @p'.

Symbolic values in tables (Figure 5) indicate relationships between tuples in tables maintained by peers @p and @p'. Algorithm 1 describes propagation of a query (more precisely, a thread of the query) stored in @$p : Queries$. The propagation mode can be either $P2P$ (a query is to be propagated to all partners with $P2P$ mode), or $local$ (a query is to be answered in the peer's data source without propagation).

Tuple $q1$ contains a query and its context (e.g. $q1.myPatt$ is a schema against which $q1.myQualif$ has been formulated). $LeadsToCycle(q1, @p')$ returns $true$ if the propagation causes a cycle, i.e. @p' occurs in $q1.qryTrace$. $discovery$ $MayBeDone(q1, @p)$ is $true$ if the hypothesis of Proposition 1 does not hold. $acceptedPropagation(q1, @p')$ is $true$ if @p' accepts the propagation of $q1$ with given parameters.

If the source peer @p' accepts a propagation $q1$ then it creates the following tuple $q2$ and inserts it into the @$p' : Queries$ table:

Algorithm 1 (*query propagation*)

Input: @p – a current peer; @p : *Peer*, @p : *Partners*,
            @p : *Queries*, @p : *Propagations* – tables on the peer @p;
Output: New states of tables @p : *Queries* and @p : *Propagations*
            if a partner peer @p' accepts the propagation.
q := @p:*Queries*; // *a row describing the query thread to be propagated*
if $q.propagMode=$'*P2P*' {
    $q1$:= **new** *propagationParametersType*;
                                // *used to prepare propagations to all partners*
    $q1.propagId$:= **new** *propagId*;
    $q1.qryThreadId$:= $q.qryThreadId$;
    $q1.qryId$:= $q.qryId$;
    $q1.qryTrace$:= $q.qryTrace + $@$p$;
                                // *the sequence of visited peers used to avoid cycles*
    $q1.myPeer$:= @p; // *the peer where the answer should be returned*
    $q1.myQualif$:= $q.myQualif$; // *the query qualifier*
    $q1.propagMode$:= "*P2P*";
    $q1.mergeMode$:= $q.mergeMode$;
    $q1.myPatt$:= @p:*Peer.myPatt*; // *the schema of* @p
    foreach @p' **in**   @p:*Partners.partPeer*
    { // *attempt to propagate the query to all partners*
        if *LeadsToCycle*($q1$, @p') **and not** *discoveryMayBeDone*($q1$, @p)
            then next
        if *LeadsToCycle*($q1$, @p') **then** $q1.propagMode$:= "*local*";
        if *acceptedPropagation*($q1$, @p') **then**
            insert into @p:*Propagations*
            values ($q1.propagId$, $q1.qryThreadId$, @p', *null*, "*Waiting*") }
}

5   Conclusions

The paper presents a method for schema mapping and query reformulation in a P2P XML data integration system. The discussed formal approach enables us to specify schemas, schema constraints, schema mappings, and queries in a uniform and precise way. We discussed some issues concerning query propagation strategies and merging modes, when missing data is to be discovered in the P2P integration processes. The approach is implemented in SixP2P system. We presented its general architecture, and sketched the way how queries and answers were sent across the P2P environment.

Acknowledgement. The work was supported in part by the Polish Ministry of Science and Higher Education under Grant N516 015 31/1553.

References

1. Abiteboul, S., Benjelloun, O., Manolescu, I., Milo, T., Weber, R.: Active XML: Peer-to-Peer Data and Web Services Integration. In: VLDB, pp. 1087–1090. Morgan Kaufmann, San Francisco (2002)
2. Abiteboul, S., Hull, R., Vianu, V.: Foundations of Databases. Addison-Wesley, Reading (1995)
3. Arenas, M.: Normalization theory for XML. SIGMOD Record 35(4), 57–64 (2006)
4. Arenas, M., Libkin, L.: XML Data Exchange: Consistency and Query Answering. In: PODS Conference, pp. 13–24 (2005)
5. Brzykcy, G., Bartoszek, J., Pankowski, T.: Schema Mappings and Agents' Actions in P2P Data Integration System. Journal of Universal Computer Science 14(7), 1048–1060 (2008)
6. Fagin, R., Kolaitis, P.G., Popa, L., Tan, W.C.: Composing Schema Mappings: Second-Order Dependencies to the Rescue. In: PODS, pp. 83–94 (2004)
7. Fuxman, A., Kolaitis, P.G., Miller, R.J., Tan, W.C.: Peer data exchange. ACM Trans. Database Syst. 31(4), 1454–1498 (2006)
8. Koloniari, G., Pitoura, E.: Peer-to-peer management of XML data: issues and research challenges. SIGMOD Record 34(2), 6–17 (2005)
9. Madhavan, J., Halevy, A.Y.: Composing Mappings Among Data Sources. In: VLDB, pp. 572–583 (2003)
10. Melnik, S., Bernstein, P.A., Halevy, A.Y., Rahm, E.: Supporting Executable Mappings in Model Management. In: SIGMOD Conference, pp. 167–178 (2005)
11. Milo, T., Abiteboul, S., Amann, B., Benjelloun, O., Ngoc, F.D.: Exchanging intensional XML data. ACM Trans. Database Syst. 30(1), 1–40 (2005)
12. Ooi, B.C., Shu, Y., Tan, K.-L.: Relational Data Sharing in Peer-based Data Management Systems. SIGMOD Record 32(3), 59–64 (2003)
13. Pankowski, T.: Reconciling inconsistent data in probabilistic XML data integration. In: Gray, A., Jeffery, K., Shao, J. (eds.) BNCOD 2008. LNCS, vol. 5071, pp. 75–86. Springer, Heidelberg (2008)
14. Pankowski, T.: XML data integration in SixP2P – a theoretical framework. In: EDBT Workshop Data Management in P2P Systems (DAMAP 2008), pp. 1–8. ACM Digital Library (2008)
15. Pankowski, T., Cybulka, J., Meissner, A.: XML Schema Mappings in the Presence of Key Constraints and Value Dependencies. In: ICDT 2007 Workshop EROW 2007, CEUR Workshop Proceedings. CEUR-WS.org, vol. 229, pp. 1–15 (2007)
16. Tatarinov, I., Halevy, A.Y.: Efficient Query Reformulation in Peer-Data Management Systems. In: SIGMOD Conference, pp. 539–550 (2004)
17. Tatarinov, I., Ives, Z.G., Madhavan, J., Halevy, A.Y., Suciu, D., Dalvi, N.N., Dong, X., Kadiyska, Y., Miklau, G., Mork, P.: The Piazza peer data management project. SIGMOD Record 32(3), 47–52 (2003)
18. XML Path Language (XPath) 2.0 (2006), http://www.w3.org/TR/xpath20
19. Yu, C., Popa, L.: Constraint-Based XML Query Rewriting For Data Integration. In: SIGMOD Conference, pp. 371–382 (2004)

Dynamic Source Selection in Large Scale Mediation Systems*

Alexandra Pomares, Claudia Roncancio, José Abásolo, and Pilar Villamil

Universidad de los Andes, Bogotá, Colombia
INP Grenoble / LIG Laboratory, France
{apomares,claudia.roncancio}@imag.fr,
{jabasolo,mavillam}@uniandes.edu.co

Abstract. This paper proposes ORS, an original strategy to reduce the number of data sources to access during query evaluation in large scale mediation systems. ORS proceeds first selecting sources using extensional (data) information to discard useless sources and then validates the intentional (schema) information that each one is able to provide. The first step is based on location queries on some "well chosen" data sources, that previously had made a consolidation integration effort. This paper proposes ORS to improve querying semantic virtual objects whose instances are distributed across numerous data sources. Cost analysis and implementation in a grid context are also presented.

Keywords: Large Scale Data Mediation, Source Selection, Distributed Source Selection.

1 Introduction

A virtual organization (VO) is a set of autonomous collaborating organizations working toward a common goal. A VO enables disparate groups to share resources [1], one of which is data. Even if there are proposals for coping with heterogeneous data in distributed contexts, they do not fully meet characteristics of data manipulation in VOs: highly distribution, high number of data sources, high data volume and autonomy which derives syntactic and semantic heterogeneity, intentional(schema) and extensional(data) overlapping. Some of those proposals ([2,3,4,5,6]) focus on query planning and execution based on the intentional (schema) level of data sources. In large scale VO such approach may imply to access useless data sources because, even if schemas match, they do not contain useful data. Others, like [7,8], limit the number of sources to access using static approaches which consider data at the extensional level. Such proposals would be better suited for large scale VO but they target contexts where there is not a large amount of data and data does not evolve very often. And in some cases like [8] the type of supported queries are restricted.

This paper proposes an original strategy called ORS (Opportunistic Referential Sources), to reduce the number of data sources to access during distributed

---

* This research is supported by Ecos-Colciencias C06M02/C07M02.

A. Hameurlain (Ed.): Globe 2008, LNCS 5187, pp. 58–69, 2008.

query processing in a wrapper-mediator architecture in large scale contexts. ORS uses source selection based on intentional (schema) information and enhances it making a previous step of sources preselection using extensional information(data) extracted from some "well chosen" data sources. Such data sources are participants as the others but are recognized as integrating referential data. Our proposal relies on an opportunistic use of such data to guide source selection. The main original characteristics of our proposal are: (1) ORS increases the accuracy of sources selection to evaluate queries with any degree of selectivity. (2) It includes a dynamic analysis of intentional and extensional data which tolerates modifications on data sources. (3) It is designed to be used in large-scale contexts.

In the following, Section 2 introduces some related work. Section 3 presents the data architecture we consider. Section 4 presents the ORS strategy. Section 5 presents a cost analysis of ORS. Section 6 discusses implementation aspects. Finally, Section 7 concludes the paper and introduces future work.

2   Related Work

Multi-sources querying has been intensively studied since more than 15 years. This section gives an overview of representative proposals and focuses on source selection for query evaluation purposes in large scale contexts. Most proposals to query autonomous heterogeneous data sources rely on mediation systems [9]. Their architecture ([10,2,3,4]) distinguishes four levels: Data sources, Wrappers, Mediation and Application level. Numerous efforts focused on the optimization of building mediation systems (as [10,11,12]) and its adaptability (as [6]).

Heterogeneity and query optimization are some of the main issues. The first issue is widely studied in [13,14,15,16,17] focus on reducing semantic heterogeneity that is not covered by wrappers. The second one has been studied using three approaches: (1) focus on minimizing communication costs based on schema distribution [18,19] using semi-joins to reduce data transfers. (2) focus on minimizing communication by reducing the number of queried sources with the help of catalogs of data[20,21] [22]) and data summaries [8,7] during query planning. And (3) focus on parallelization techniques to improve response time [23,24]. These proposals introduced major advances in mediation of heterogeneous sources. However, the adaptation of such optimization strategies to large scale contexts is not well treated. This paper deals with query optimization through the reduction of the number of queried sources. Methods to select data sources that rely only on schema matching and evaluation of wrappers capabilities are clearly not scalable. The reason is that subqueries are sent to all sources that match the attributes specified in the original query, without taking into account that only a few of them have instances that meet query predicates (query conditions). Approaches that reduce queried sources using static catalogs are not viable due to the autonomy and large amount of data that difficult their maintenance. Approaches using summaries are difficult to maintain up to date and only enhances a group of users queries.

3 Data Architecture

Our work concerns large scale mediation systems (see Figure 1) with three levels of data abstraction: **Local Level** is conformed by the set of shared data sources. **External Level** consists of a set of schemas defining semantic virtual objects. Multiple external schemas may exist. Instances of one virtual object may be distributed over data sources. **Conceptual Level** represents the world through a semantic and general definition of data using a domain ontology. It does not consider neither specific needs of some groups of users nor restrictions of local models. Schemas of the external level are defined as views over the domain ontology of the conceptual level called virtual objects. To modify or to create a new virtual object for a group of users, it is just required to define a new view over the domain ontology. Following, there is a portion of the virtual object *Patient* definition. It is expressed as a view over a health domain ontology in SPARQL [25]. A query in SPARQL is defined as triple patterns called basic graph pattern, where subject, predicate and object may be a variable. The answer of a SPARQL query is a subgraph of the ontology data that matches with the pattern.

Virtual Object Patient: SELECT ?ActType ?EntityName, ?Address ? MaritalStat, ?BirthTime WHERE{?Act :classAct ?ActType. ?Act :hasParticipation ?Participation. ?Participation :executes ?Role. ?Role :player ?Entity. ?Entity :desc ?EntityName. ?Entity :addr ?Address. ?Entity :maritalStatus ?MaritalStat. ?Entity :birthTime ?BirthTime. ?Role :classRol ?ClassCode.FILTER regex(?ClassRol,"Patient")}

User queries are formulated over a virtual object definition, adding the convenient group of filters to retrieve the desired instances. Query is translated to local schemas and finally executed on data sources at the local level.

Relationships between organizations that produce data sources can give rise to relationships among sources. For example, sources from organization A may

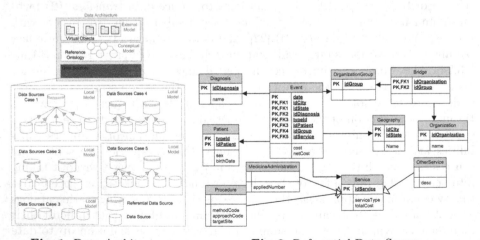

Fig. 1. Data Architecture   **Fig. 2.** Referential Data Source

contain summary data of sources from organizations B, C and D due to an actual regulatory relationship. The explicit or implicit knowledge contained in A with respect to the original location of data can be useful to reduce the effort to find the sources that must participate in a distributed query.

In the local level a data source is called a Referential Data Source (RDS) if it is able to provide location knowledge for the instances of one or more virtual objects and it declares the way to extract this knowledge in the form of Location Query. An RDS can be used opportunistically to obtain location data to resolve a user query. This is the basis of our proposal called *Opportunistic Referential Sources (ORS)* strategy, presented in detail in Section 4.

The assumption of the existence of relationships between data sources is based on the analysis of different VOs. In particular, the analysis of health VOs threw an important number of relationships as a consequence of two factors: (1)regulatory and administrative processes, and (2)cooperation between health care service providers with the agencies to combat diseases like cancer, AIDS, diabetes, etc. In general, the analysis of data environments from VOs allowed us to conclude that relationships during operative processes and the execution of services to the same individual (eg. clients, proteins, institutions) cause different kinds of relationships inter-sources.

Figure 2 shows a RDS in a health VO with information about patients. There is a fact table representing cost measures of a given service delivered to a patient in a geographic place and executed by a group of organizations. In this RDS, location data about instances of patient can be obtained querying the dimension organization (organization group, bridge and organization) joined with the dimension *Patient*. The Location Query for the virtual object Patient in this RDS is formulated in SPARQL [25]. The WHERE clause provides the basic graph pattern to match against the domain ontology.

Location Query: *SELECT ?instanceId ?orgId WHERE {?Entidad :code ?InstanceId. ?Entity :playerRole ?Role. ?Role :isExecuted ?Participation. ?Participation :participates ?Encounter. ?Entity2 :code ?orgId. ?Entity2 :playerRole ?Role2. ?Role2 :isExecuted ?Participation2. ?Participation2 :participates ?Encounter. ?Role :classRol ?ClassCode. FILTER regex(?ClassCode,"Patient")}*

4   ORS Data Source Selection Strategy

Processing a virtual object query implies to materialize instances that satisfy user requirements. Source selection becomes a critical process because the distribution of each instance data can be different. This section presents ORS, a strategy to reduce the number of accessed data sources during query evaluation in large scale mediation systems. Section 4.1 presents an overview of ORS strategy. Section 4.2 and 4.3 present respectively the extensional and intentional evaluation process during query planning. Section 4.4 discusses ORS with several data source scenarios.

4.1   Overview

ORS reduces the number of queried data sources to only those relevant for a user query. Let Qu(v,ReqElem(e1..en), Filter(e1 op Val,..,em op Val)) be a user query. A source is relevant to Qu iff it satisfies Qu intentionally and extensionally:

– Intentional Satisfaction: (1) Data source schema contains one element mapped to the identification property of the virtual object v. (2) Data source schema includes at least one element *(ei)* used in Qu
– Extensional Satisfaction: (1) Data source contains at least one instance of v that satisfies at least one filter *(ek)*.

To express the notion of source relevance during query processing we introduce the concepts of Instance and Query Cartography: for a given instance I, its cartography[26] Ic designates the set of nodes containing data about it. For a given query Q, its cartography Qc designates the set of Ic of the instances on the answer of Q. ORS is in charge of obtain Qc during query planning and deliver it to enrich the query evaluation phase.

Figure 3 illustrates query processing using the ORS strategy. Query Planning input are the user query Qu and the set of Location queries $Ql's$ of RDSs available in the system. *Extensional evaluation* makes the fusion between $Ql's$ and Qu to obtain location information from available RDSs. It also evaluates extensional overlapping of sources using the declared relationship between sources that describes how their content is related (inclusion, intersection, complement). The result is an incomplete query cartography $Qc\alpha$ that contains the set of relevant instances ids and the sources containing data about them. If there is a filter that was not possible to evaluate, this phase also includes this filter (ej) as an output. *Intentional Evaluation* takes $Qc\alpha$, evaluates the intentional ability of data sources to answer Qu and validates the intentional overlapping between sources. It adds the properties that each data source is able to provide to $Qc\alpha$ and associates to the unresolved filter(s) ej the sources that are able to resolve it. The result is the complete Qc with not redundant sources and the set of sources that can resolve filter ej.

Query Evaluation inputs are Qc and the unresolved filter(s)[ej] with the sources able to resolve it. The task of *Distributed Execution* is to deliver the

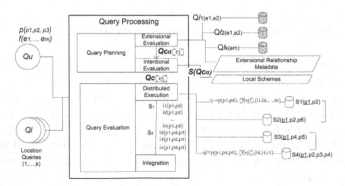

Fig. 3. ORS Strategy

subqueries to the related local sources. Each source receives a query with (1) the properties that is able to resolve, (2) optionally the unresolved filters during query planning (if the source is able to resolve it) and (3) a filter condition to obtain only the properties for the instances id's related in Qc. *Integration* phase takes local answers, validates which of them are possible to integrate (due to data relationship between sources) and makes the integration.

4.2   Extensional Evaluation

The goal is to identify the extensional data that each source is able to provide to evaluate a Qu. The output is the list of relevant instances Ri's for Qu associated with the sources that contain data about them and the group of unresolved filters. The following tasks are executed:

a. Add the Filters of the Virtual Object Query to the Location Query. The location query obtains the ids of all the instances that are into a RDS associated with a set of locations ids. Nevertheless, to resolve a query we only need the instances ids that match the filters of the user query. For the virtual object *Patient* (definition in section sub:Data-Architecture), a filter to obtain all the patients associated with medical procedures is:**FILTER***regex (?ActType, " Procedure")}*.

With the location query and the virtual object query, both expressed in terms of the domain ontology, it is necessary to integrate them to restrict the basic graph pattern of the location query to obtain only the Ri's. The goal of this task is to handle this "query heterogeneity" to execute the location query and obtains only Ri's. Algorithm 1 shows the strategy to make this "fusion".

Algorithm 1. Query Analysis and Reformulation

```
Input:  L Location Query, B Virtual Object Query
Output: Location query with the Virtual Object Query filters
Begin
   L'= L
   Pl= GetPredicates( L)   //name, domain and range of each predicate of L
   Pb= GetPredicates(B)    //name, domain and range of each predicate of B
   While(Filters in B)
      f = getFilter(L)     // The value of the filter is assigned to f
      v = getFilterVariable(f)  // v is the variable of the filter
      vd = getDomains(v,Pl) // domain of triplets where v acts as a ?subject
      vr = getRanges(v,Pb)  // domain of triplets where v acts as an ?object
      c = Intersect(vd,vr)  // name of classes which define the variable v
      cn = ObtainNamedClasses(c, L, Pl)  // given name to the class c in L
      Filter = ModifyQuerySection(B,f,cn) //Modifies ?subject and ?object
                                 where f was involved
      L' = AddFilterTriple(L, Filter)    //Adds the needed new triplets for
                         make consistent the query L' with  the new filter
      L'= AddFilter(f)                   //Adds the new set of filters to L'
   End While
   Return(L')
End
```

If there are RDSs that are not able to resolve all the filters, an initial evaluation of filters knowledge is made using the intentional definition of each RDS. This determines if there is a mapping between the filter property and RDS schema and maintains a registry of which filters were not possible to evaluate in each RDS (unresolved filters), to resolve them directly on data sources.

b. Execute the Transformed Query. To execute a transformed location query means to convert the query expressed in ontology terms into a query in the native query language of the referential data source. This transformation is in charge of the wrapper level of the mediation system. For Health VO for example, taking the structure of the Social Security datawarehouse (figure 2), the conversion of the location query into a SQL query is the following:

Transformed Location Query in Native Source Language: Select p.idPatient, b.idOrganization From Patient p Join Event e On p.typeid=e.typeid and p.idPatient = e.idPAtient Join OrganizationGroup o On e.idGroup= o.idGroup Join Bridge b On o.idGroup=b.idGroup Join Diagnosis d On e.idDiagnosis = d.idDiagnosis where d.name = "Diabetes"

The answer is: *{(InstanceId1, idOrganizationIdk),..., (InstanceId1, idOrganization-Idn), ...,(InstanceIdn, idOrganizationIdl),..., (InstanceIdn, idOrganizationIdm)}*,

where idOrganization represents a data source or a group of data sources. In the last case, is necessary to make an additional step to determine which is the relevant data source related to idOrganization.

c. Initial Query Cartography Creation. Since data to create an instance can be provided by more than one data source, this phase determines which is the group of sources necessary and sufficient to create instances related to Qu. The declaration of extensional overlapping between sources is used to accomplish this task. The possible relationships supported by ORS at this moment are: intersection $\{VDO, A \cap B, [(p_i, ope, val)]\}$, complement $\{VDO, A' = B, [(p_i, ope, val)]\}$ and inclusion $\{VDO, A \subset B, [(p_i, ope, val)]\}$. The optional element means that the relationship applies only to the group of VDO instances that match to the condition where p is a property, op is an operator and val is a value or an expression. The strategy consists in reduce the number of sources beginning with those obtained from the location queries in the available RDSs. The first phase of the algorithm evaluates the group of data sources that have a relationship. This phase generates three groups. Each one with the potential data sources to remove as a result of the corresponding relationship. The second phase combines the results of each group and leaves the data sources that minimize a cost function. At this moment all data sources increase the cost function uniformly. Nevertheless, it can be included network cost or monetary cost.

4.3   Intentional Cartography Generation

This phase takes instance Ids related to locations, obtained in the preceding phase, and uses the intentional information of sources to eliminate those do not match intentionally with the query. Query Cartography at this moment includes the portion of the original query that each source is able to resolve to materialize the required instance(s) including the filters that were not evaluated during query planning. This phase selects the local views that have to be used to execute the query in each data source as traditional GAV approach using the mapping metadata obtained during data sources registration. Subsequently, the distributed execution process plans the distribution of materialization of each instance (or a group of instances), accordingly to the physical state (node availability, node processing capacity, node cost, etc.). If physical state evaluation informs that one data source referred in the query cartography is unavailable, the strategy allows to deliver an incomplete answer, informing which are the unreachable data sources and which instances were affected.

4.4 Data Sources Scenarios

When there is only one RDS, cartography creation relies on the use of data provided therein. However, not all VOs have the same scenario of local data (Figure 1). In all the cases, it could be possible to apply the strategy with additional steps. For instance, when there are several RDSs (cases 2, 4 and 5), there has to be added a step that integrates the cartographies obtained from each RDS. If additionally, there is overlapping between RDS, it is necessary to add a step where the cartographies obtained from each one are intersect with the cartography of the others (cases 4 and 5). When there are sources that are not referred in any referential source (case 5), its intentional data is used to select it or not in the execution of a query.

Knowledge contained in RDS about query filters can be variable. If all the filters are evaluated during query planning, the integration of subqueries answers is made directly. On the contrary, during intentional evaluation the unresolved filter is included to all subqueries that will be executed on a source that is able to resolve it. This step assures that all the instances obtained from them are completely coherent to the query. Next, during integration phase, the instances for which all the filters were evaluated are grouped as "Guaranteed" instances, those for which were evaluated only a subgroup of filters are not delivered to the user or are delivered as "Not Guaranteed".

5 Query Evaluation Costs

The evaluation of ORS focuses on the measure of the actual reduction of sources to access during query evaluation and the overhead introduced during query planning. This section presents an overview of this and compares it with metrics obtained following a strategy based on a model "Global as View" (GAV)[10] that only uses intentional metadata to select target sources. Following we present variables involved during the analysis of each metric:

Nds: number of nodes with data sources	**Nrs:** number of nodes with RDSs	**Vn:** number of virtual object instances.
Pv: number of properties of a virtual object	**Pq:** number of properties selected in a query.	**Sq:** size in bytes of a query
Sl: size in bytes of location information of a property	**Rs:** size in bytes of source relationship description	**Ls:** size in bytes of query limitations capacity description
Sel: selectivity factor of a query.	**Sp:** size in bytes of a virtual object property	**Sv:** size in bytes of an empty message
Et: percentage of data distribution of virtual object instances over data sources	**It:** percentage of schema distribution of virtual object over data sources	**Df:** It is the known duplication % of queried instances due sources relationship

Storage Space. (*CSP*) represents the space required by a node to support source selection strategy.

$$CSP_{GAV} = \overbrace{\sum_{i=1}^{Nds} Ls_i}^{SourceCapabilities}. \tag{1}$$

$$CSP_{ORS} = \sum_{i=1}^{Nds} \left(\overbrace{Ls_i}^{SourceCapabilities} + \overbrace{Rs_i}^{SourceRelationship} \right) + \overbrace{\sum_{i=1}^{Nrs} Sq_i}^{LocationQuery}. \tag{2}$$

Planning Network Messaging. (*CNP*) represents the volume of data the system has to exchange to plan the query.

$$CNP_{ORS} = \overbrace{\sum_{i=1}^{Nrs} Sq_i}^{LocationQuery} + \overbrace{\sum_{j=1}^{Pv} (Sl_j).Sel.Vn}^{AnswerToLocationQuery}. \tag{3}$$

Execution Network Messaging. (*CNE*) represents the volume of data transfered during the evaluation of a query.

$$CNE_{GAV} \overbrace{\sum_{i=1}^{Nds.It} (Sq_i)}^{QueryMessages} + \overbrace{(1+Df).\sum_{i=1}^{Pq} (Sp_i).Sel.Vn}^{VirtualObjectInstances} + \overbrace{(Sv.(It-Et).Nds)}^{EmptyAnswers}. \tag{4}$$

$$CNE_{ORS} = \overbrace{\sum_{i=1}^{Nds.Et} (Sq_i)}^{QueryMessages} + \overbrace{\sum_{i=1}^{Pq} (Sp_i).Sel.Vn}^{VirtualObjectsInstances}. \tag{5}$$

Queried Nodes. (*Qn*) represents the total number of nodes that are queried during query processing (planning and execution). The comparison distinguishes two types of sources: *Useful*, those returning data relevant to a query. *Useless* return empty answers.

$$Qn_{GAV} = \overbrace{Nds.Et}^{UsefulNodes} + \overbrace{Nds.(It-Et)}^{UselessNodes}. \tag{6}$$

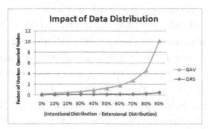

Fig. 4. Impact of Data Distribution   **Fig. 5.** GainComparison

$$
Qn_{ORS} = \overbrace{(1 - Df).(Nrs + Nds.Et)}^{UsefulNodes} + \overbrace{0.}^{UselessNodes} \tag{7}
$$

Evaluation of query execution using ORS approach includes tests with 1000 nodes, 20 RDSs, 500.000 distributed instances of virtual objects, a query with 10% of selectivity and different levels of extensional and intentional distribution of virtual objects.

Figure 4 shows how the difference between intentional and extensional distribution affects the behavior of both strategies. The factor of useless queried nodes represents the increment on the proportion of nodes that are queried and do not contain relevant data. The increment in ORS is due to the RDSs that can be queried during planning and do not provide instances relevant for the query. Figure 5 shows gain with respect to GAV approach for each metric during the execution of three tests changing extensional and intentional distribution of queried instances.

ORS strategy proves to be a better option when the proportion between intentional and extensional distribution is high. Although ORS implies an increase in storage and network use during query planning, it enhances query evaluation. Depending on the difference between extensional and intentional distribution, the reduction in the number of nodes may not be as significant among the strategies. However, even if the reduction is minimal, the ability to know apriori what sources have relevant data guarantees higher quality responses ensuring completeness on the answer or informed incomplete answers (see section 4.4).

6   Prototype: ARIBEC

The ORS strategy was implemented within a large scale mediation system, called ARIBEC. It adopts a service-oriented architecture and provides four groups of services: *Application services*, responsible for the creation and launch of queries on virtual objects and system configuration; *Mediation services* responsible for planning and execution of queries that origin the creation of objects instances materialized on demand; ORS is a mediation service. *Wrapping services* that guarantee the resolution of schematic and syntactic heterogeneity problems, delivering standardized data; *Security services* which allow registration in the system and guarantee the confidentiality of data anywhere it goes.

ARIBEC is an OGSA-compliant system, data sources and services are exposed as grid services. Services expose a standard interface built around WSDL source descriptions, and relevant services communicate using SOAP messages. The prototype is in Java 1.5 and we used Globus Toolkit 4.0.3. Data sources are exposed via OGSA-DAI WSRF version 2.2. To assist wrapping services we use the D2RQ engine [27] that provides a language to describe mappings between relational DB and ontologies in OWL/ RDFS and a service to evaluate SPARQL queries on a relational DB. The prototype is under test. The next phase will focus on its deployment on a grid and on performance testing.

7   Conclusions and Future Work

This paper presents ORS, a new source selection strategy to improve query evaluation involving distributed sources in large scale contexts. The principle is to improve mediation using opportunistically integration efforts already made following the consolidation technique. To the best of our knowledge, this is the first attempt to support distributed queries using this approach.

ORS was designed to be used in contexts where there is at least one referential data source. It is effective when the proportion of intentional distribution is higher than the extensional distribution, making useful to reduce the number of sources using the location data. It improves the evaluation of queries that involve filters with high selectivity and guarantees the dynamic adaptability of the system, as relevant sources are identified at query evaluation time. Even when the difference between intentional and extensional distribution is minimal, the strength of ORS is the ability to know apriori what sources have relevant data assuring higher quality responses and completeness on the response.

Our strategy is part of a large scale mediation system deployed on grid infrastructure. The prototype is under test. Short term work involves large scale experiments and performance comparisons. We are also interested in scenarios where there are not "natural" RDS using: a strategy based on distributed semantic caching [28] and detailed data summaries that can act as artificial RDS. We will also further study the impact of the number and completeness of RDS.

References

1. Foster, I., Kesselman, C., Tuecke, S.: The anatomy of the grid: Enabling scalable virtual organizations. Int. J. High Perform. Comput. Appl. 15, 200–222 (2001)
2. Roth, M., Schwarz, P.: A wrapper architecture for legacy data sources. In: Proc. vldb conference (1997)
3. Tomasic, A., Raschid, L., Valduriez, P.: Scaling access to heterogeneous data sources with DISCO. Knowledge and Data Engineering 10, 808–823 (1998)
4. Kossmann, D.: The state of the art in distributed query processing. ACM Comput. Surv. 32, 422–469 (2000)
5. Melnik, S., et al.: A mediation infrastructure for digital library services. In: DL 2000: Fifth ACM conference on Digital libraries, pp. 123–132. ACM Press, New York (2000)

6. Bruno, G., Collet, C., Vargas-Solar, G.: Configuring intelligent mediators using ontologies. In: EDBT Workshops, pp. 554–572 (2006)
7. Bleiholder, J., et al.: Query planning in the presence of overlapping sources. In: Grust, T., Höpfner, H., Illarramendi, A., Jablonski, S., Mesiti, M., Müller, S., Patranjan, P.-L., Sattler, K.-U., Spiliopoulou, M., Wijsen, J. (eds.) EDBT 2006. LNCS, vol. 4254, pp. 811–828. Springer, Heidelberg (2006)
8. Yu, B., et al.: Effective keyword-based selection of relational databases. In: SIGMOD 2007, pp. 139–150. ACM, New York (2007)
9. Wiederhold, G.: Mediators in the architecture of future information systems. Computer 25, 38–49 (1992)
10. Garcia-Molina, H., et al.: The tsimmis approach to mediation: Data models and languages. Journal of Intelligent Information Systems 8, 117–132 (1997)
11. Stevens, R., et al.: Tambis: Transparent access to multiple bioinformatics information sources. Bioinformatics 16, 184–186 (2000)
12. Doan, A., et al.: Reconciling schemas of disparate data sources: a machine-learning approach. In: SIGMOD 2001, pp. 509–520. ACM Press, New York (2001)
13. Gounaris, A., et al.: A service-oriented system to support data integration on data grids. In: CCGRID 2007, pp. 627–635. IEEE Computer Society, Los Alamitos (2007)
14. Wang, Q., Chen, J., Gao, X., Zhou, W., Yan, B.: A new architecture of data access middleware under grid environment. apscc 0, 384–391 (2006)
15. Liu, J., Wu, Y., Zheng, W.: Grid enabled data integration framework for bioinformatics research. In: GCC Workshops, pp. 401–406 (2006)
16. Wöhrer, A., Brezany, P., Tjoa, A.M.: Novel mediator architectures for grid information systems. Future Gener. Comput. Syst. 21, 107–114 (2005)
17. Wenlong, H., et al.: Data model and virtual database engine for grid environment. In: GCC 2007, pp. 823–829. IEEE Computer Society, Los Alamitos (2007)
18. Apers, P.M.G., Hevner, A.R., Yao, S.B.: Optimization algorithms for distributed queries, 262–273 (1986)
19. Haraty, R.A., Fany, R.C.: Query acceleration in distributed database systems. Revista Comlombiana de Computación 2, 19–34 (2001)
20. Levy, A.Y., et al.: Querying heterogeneous information sources using source descriptions. In: VLDB, Bombay, India, VLDB Endowment, pp. 251–262 (1996)
21. Duschka, O.M., Genesereth, M.R.: Query planning in infomaster. In: Selected Areas in Cryptography, pp. 109–111 (1997)
22. Nie, T., et al.: Sla-based data integration on database grids. In: COMPSAC (2), pp. 613–618 (2007)
23. Liu, C., Chen, H.: A hash partition strategy for distributed query processing. In: Extending Database Technology, pp. 373–387 (1996)
24. Gounaris, A., et al.: A novel approach to resource scheduling for parallel query processing on computational grids. Distrib. Parallel Databases 19, 87–106 (2006)
25. Eric Prud'hommeaux, A.S.: Sparql query language for rdf (2007), http://www.w3.org/tr/rdf-sparql-query/
26. Verdier, C.: Health information systems: from local to pervasive medical data. Santé et Systémique 9, 87–108 (2006)
27. Berlin, F.U.: The d2rq plattform (2007), http://sites.wiwiss.fu-berlin.de/suhl/bizer/d2rq/
28. d'Orazio, L., et al.: Distributed semantic caching in grid middleware. In: Wagner, R., Revell, N., Pernul, G. (eds.) DEXA 2007. LNCS, vol. 4653, pp. 162–171. Springer, Heidelberg (2007)

Information Sharing Agents in a Peer Data Exchange System

Leopoldo Bertossi[1] and Loreto Bravo[2]

[1] Carleton University, School of Computer Science, Ottawa, Canada
bertossi@scs.carleton.ca
[2] University of Edinburgh, School of Informatics, Edinburgh, UK
lbravo@inf.ed.ac.uk

Abstract. We present a semantics and answer set programs for relational *peer data exchange systems*. When a peer answers a query, it exchanges data with other peers in order to supplement or modify its own data source. The data exchange relationships between peers are specified by logical sentences called *data exchange constraints* and *trust relationships*, which together determine how data is moved around (in order to keep them satisfied). This process determines virtual, alternative instances for a peer that can be specified as the models of an answer set program. The *peer consistent answers* to a query that are returned by a peer are those that are invariant under all these instances. The logic program can be used to compute peer consistent answers.

1 Introduction

A peer data exchange system (PDES) can be seen as a set of information agents, each of them being the owner of a data source. When one of them receives a query, in order to answer it, its data is completed or modified according to relevant data that the other agents may have. More precisely, a peer data exchange system (PDES) is a finite set $\mathcal{P} = \{P_1, \ldots P_n\}$ of peers, each of them with a local relational database instance. A peer P may be directly related to another peer P' by means of a set $\Sigma(P, P')$ of *data exchange constraints* (DECs), which are first-order sentences expressed in terms of the two participating database schemas. DECs between two peers are expected to be satisfied by the combination of the two local instances.[1] However, this condition is taken into account only when local queries are answered. That is, each peer will not update its physical instance according to its DECs and other peers' instances. Instead, if a peer P is answering a query, it may, at query time import data from other peers to complement its data and/or ignore part of its own data. In which way a peer uses the data from other peers depends on its DECs, the peers' instances, and its *trust relationships* to other peers: a peer P may trust its data the same as or less than other peers' data.

In this paper we present in simple terms and by means of examples a formal semantics for such a system of peers who exchange data for query answering. The

---

[1] For simplicity, but without loss of generality, local schemas are pairwise disjoint.

A. Hameurlain (Ed.): Globe 2008, LNCS 5187, pp. 70–81, 2008.

most important role of a semantics in this case is to characterize in precise terms
what are the intended and correct answers to a query posed to and answered
by a peer in the system. We propose a *model-theoretic semantics*, that is a
collection of possible and admissible models over which the system is interpreted.
The expected answers from a peer to a query are those that are *certain* wrt a
set of database instances associated to that peer. Furthermore, our declarative
semantics can be made executable, by using logic programs with stable model
semantics [12] to specify the intended models. The precise formal semantics was
presented in detailed technical terms in [3].

If for peer P it holds $\Sigma(\mathrm{P}, \mathrm{P}') \neq \emptyset$, i.e. there are DECs from P to P', we say
that P' is a *neighbor* of P. Clearly, DECs for a peer P can be *inconsistent* wrt
(not satisfied by) the combination of its instance and those of its neighbors. A
virtual combined instance for P that solves these inconsistencies by performing
a minimal set of changes on the database relations is called a *neighborhood
solution instance* for P. By restricting it to the schema of P, we get a *solution
instance* for P. There might be more than one solution instance for a peer, and
all of them are taken into consideration when answering queries posed to P: The
peer consistent answers from P are those that are shared (or returned) by all
the different solution instances. That is, a cautions (a.k.a. skeptical or certain)
semantics is applied to query answering.

Each peer P can be seen as an ontology consisting of the database instance
plus metadata that describes the database schema, local integrity constraints
(ICs), its set $\Sigma(\mathrm{P}) = \bigcup_{\mathrm{P}' \in \mathcal{P}} \Sigma(\mathrm{P}, \mathrm{P}')$ of DECs, and its trust relationships. These
ontologies may be pairwise inconsistent due to the DECs and the database facts.
We could easily extend our framework to handle DECs that contain views, i.e.
defined relational predicates. This kind of consistency issues also emerge when
aligning ontologies [13]. Our notion of DEC corresponds to concept inclusion in
the ontological scenario. However, the DECs we can handle can be much more
general than inclusions. In our case, it has to be emphasized that, whenever
possible, inconsistencies are solved at query time.

Example 1. Peers P1 and P2 have relational schemas $\mathcal{R}(\mathrm{P1}) = \{R^1, S^1\}$, $\mathcal{R}(\mathrm{P2}) = \{R^2, S^2\}$, resp. Here, P1 is connected to peer P2 by $\Sigma(\mathrm{P1}, \mathrm{P2}) = \{\forall xy(R^2(x, y) \wedge S^2(y, z) \rightarrow R^1(x, y, z)), \forall x(S^1(x) \rightarrow S^2(5, x))\}$, and it trusts P2 more than itself.

If a query is posed to P1, it has to adjust its own data so that the DECs with
P2 are satisfied. To check the satisfaction, peer P1 will ask P2 for its data. Since P2
has no DECs with other peers, it will return to P1 its physical data, without any
modification. Here, the data in P1 together with the data in P2 do not to satisfy
the first DEC. In general, such an inconsistency could be solved by virtually
removing $\langle d, 5\rangle$ from R^2 or $\langle 5, 3\rangle$ from S^2, or inserting $\langle d, 5, 3\rangle$ into R^1. But,

since P1 trusts more the data of P2, the natural choice is to add $\langle d, 5, 3 \rangle$ to R^1. In the same way, the inconsistency wrt the second DEC is solved by virtually removing tuple $\langle 7 \rangle$ from S^1. In this case, there is only one neighborhood solution (instance) centered around P1:

P1

R^1			S^1
c	4	2	3
f	3	5	
d	5	3	

P2

R^2		S^2	
c	4	4	2
d	5	5	3

Its restriction to P1 is the solution instance for P1, and it is used to answer the queries posed to P1. Thus, the query $Q_1(x) : \exists yz R^1(x, y, z)$ returns $\{\langle c \rangle, \langle f \rangle, \langle d \rangle\}$.

If we modify this example by making P1 trust P2 as much as itself, there are several possible solutions for P1, obtained by virtually modifying both peers' data. The inconsistencies wrt the first DEC would be solved by either removing $\langle d, 5 \rangle$ from R^2, or $\langle 5, 3 \rangle$ from S^2 or inserting $\langle d, 5, 3 \rangle$ into R^1, and the inconsistencies wrt the second DEC would be solved by either removing $\langle 7 \rangle$ from S^1 or inserting $\langle 5, 7 \rangle$ into S^2. There are six neighborhood solutions:

P1

R^1			S^1
c	4	2	
f	3	5	

P2

R^2		S^2	
c	4	4	2
d	5		

P1

R^1			S^1
c	4	2	7
f	3	5	
d	5	7	

P2

R^2		S^2	
c	4	4	2
d	5	5	7

P1

R^1			S^1
c	4	2	3
f	3	5	7

P2

R^2		S^2	
c	4	4	2
		5	3
		5	7

P1

R^1			S^1
c	4	2	3
f	3	5	

P2

R^2		S^2	
c	4	4	2
		5	3

P1

R^1			S^1
c	4	2	3
f	3	5	
d	5	3	

P2

R^2		S^2	
c	4	4	2
d	5	5	3

P1

R^1			S^1
c	4	2	3
f	3	5	7
d	5	3	

P2

R^2		S^2	
c	4	4	2
d	5	5	3
		5	7

In the first neighborhood solution, $\langle 5, 3 \rangle$ was removed from S^2 to solve the first inconsistency. This created a new inconsistency wrt the second DEC, which was solved by removing $\langle 3 \rangle$ from S^1.

The expected answers to query $Q_1(x)$ would now be $\langle c \rangle, \langle f \rangle$, that are the usual answers to $Q_1(x)$ shared by the six solutions for P1.   □

The definition of a solution instance for P may suggest that P can physically change other peers' data, but this is not the case. Actually, the notion of solution is used as an auxiliary notion to characterize the semantically correct answers from P's point of view. We try to avoid as much as possible the generation of material solutions instances, and ideally, P should be able to obtain its peer consistent answers just by querying the already available local instances. This resembles the approach to *consistent query answering* (CQA) in databases (cf. [4] for a survey): consistent answers to a query posed to a database that may be inconsistent wrt to certain ICs are those that are invariant under all *repairs*, i.e. the minimally repaired and consistent versions of the original instance. There are mechanisms for computing consistent answers that avoid or minimize the physical generation of repairs. In this paper, we show how disjunctive logic programs with stable models semantics [12] (or answer set programs) can be used to characterize and obtain peer consistent answers.

This paper is based on [3], which considerably extends and develops the semantics first suggested in [2]. To simplify and shorten the presentation we do not consider here local ICs, DECs with existential quantifiers nor null values in database instances. We refer to [3] for these extensions and for a general treatment of the subject.

2   A Semantics for PDESs

We assume that each peer P owns a database instance $D(P)$ conforming to a schema $\mathcal{R}(P)$, and $\mathcal{R}(P) \cap \mathcal{R}(Q) = \emptyset$ for $P \neq Q$. The schemas determine FO languages, e.g. $\mathcal{L}(P)$, $\mathcal{L}(P, Q)$. Each peer P, has a collection of (possibly empty) sets $\Sigma(P, Q)$ of sentences of $\mathcal{L}(P, Q)$, which contain the DECs from P to peer Q. It could be $\Sigma(P, Q) \neq \Sigma(Q, P)$. $\Sigma(P) := \bigcup_Q \Sigma(P, Q)$. There is also a relation *trust* $\subseteq \mathcal{P} \times \{less, same\} \times \mathcal{P}$, with exactly one triple of the form $\langle P, \cdot, Q \rangle$ for each non empty $\Sigma(P, Q)$. P owns (or stores) those triples of the form $\langle P, \cdot, \cdot \rangle$. The intended semantics of $\langle P, less(same), Q \rangle \in trust$ is that P trusts itself less than (the same as) Q. Here, we assume $\Sigma(P, P) = \emptyset$ (otherwise, see [3]).

A *universal data exchange constraint* (UDEC) between peers P, Q is a first-order (FO) sentence of the form:

$$\forall \bar{x}(\bigwedge_{i=1}^{n} R_i(\bar{x}_i) \longrightarrow (\bigvee_{j=1}^{m} Q_j(\bar{y}_j) \vee \varphi)), \tag{1}$$

where the R_i, Q_j are relations in $\mathcal{R}(P) \cup \mathcal{R}(Q)$, φ is a formula containing built-in atoms[2] only, and $\bar{x}_i, \bar{y}_j \subseteq \bar{x}$.

Query answering is, informally, as follows: When a peer P is posed a query in its local language $\mathcal{L}(P)$, it may have to determine, on the basis of its DECs, if its neighbors have data that is relevant to answer the query. So, it submits queries to its neighbors, whose answers may be used to answer the original query. However, before answering the query, P has to locally solve inconsistencies wrt to its DECs, its own data, and the data imported from the other peers. Inconsistencies are solved taking into account P's trust relationships. This leads to a set of virtual instances, the minimal repairs of P's local instance previously extended with its peers' data. In them, together with the neighbors' instances, P's DECs are

---

[2] For example, $x = 5$, $y \neq z$ and $z < 2$.

satisfied. The answers returned by P to the user are those that are true in the restrictions to $\mathcal{R}(\text{P})$ of all those instances.

As expected, the solution instances for a peer will be determined not only by its relationships with its neighbors, but also by the neighbors of its neighbors, etc. An *accessibility graph* $\mathcal{G}(\mathcal{P})$ can be used to represent the connections via DECs between peers. It contains a vertex for each peer $\text{P} \in \mathcal{P}$ and a directed edge from Pi to Pj if $\Sigma(\text{Pi}, \text{Pj}) \neq \emptyset$. An edge from Pi to Pj is labeled with "<" when $\langle \text{Pi}, less, \text{Pj} \rangle \in trust$, or with "=" when $\langle \text{Pi}, same, \text{Pj} \rangle \in trust.$[3] P' is *accessible* from P if there is a path in $\mathcal{G}(\mathcal{P})$ from P to P' or P'=P. P' is a *neighbor* of P if there is an edge from P to P'. With $\mathcal{AC}(\text{P})$ and $\mathcal{N}(\text{P})$ we denote the sets of peers that are accessible from P and the neighbors of P including P itself, respectively. $\mathcal{G}(\text{P})$ is the restriction of $\mathcal{G}(\mathcal{P})$ to $\mathcal{AC}(\text{P})$.

Example 2 (extension of example 1). The DECs are $\Sigma(\text{P1}, \text{P2}) = \{\forall xyz \ (R^2(x,y) \wedge S^2(y,z) \rightarrow R^1(x,y,z)), \ \forall x \ (S^1(x) \rightarrow S^2(5,x))\}$, $\Sigma(\text{P2}, \text{P3}) = \{\forall xy \ (S^2(x,y) \rightarrow R^3(x,y))\}$, and $\Sigma(\text{P4}, \text{P3}) = \{\forall xyz \ (R^3(x,y) \rightarrow R^4(x,y,3))\}$. Here, $\mathcal{N}(\text{P1}) = \{\text{P1}, \text{P2}\}$.

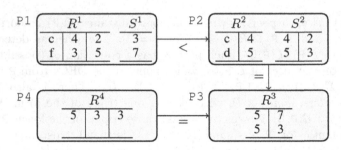

If a query is posed to P1, it will send queries to P2, to check the satisfaction of the DECs in $\Sigma(\text{P1}, \text{P2})$. But, in order for P2 to answer those queries, it will send queries to peer P3 to check the DECs in $\Sigma(\text{P2}, \text{P3})$. Since P3 is not connected to any other peer, it will answer P2's queries using its material instance $D(\text{P3})$. Thus, the solutions for P1 and the peer consistent answers from P1 will be affected by the peers in $\mathcal{AC}(\text{P1}) = \{\text{P1}, \text{P2}, \text{P3}\}$. Solutions for P4 will be affected by $\mathcal{AC}(\text{P4}) = \{\text{P4}, \text{P3}\}$. $\square$

The data distributed across different peers has to be appropriately gathered to build solution instances for a peer, and different semantics may emerge as candidates, depending on the granularity of the data sent between peers. Here we present one according to which the data that a peer P receives from a neighbor Q to build its own solutions is the *intersection of the solutions* for Q. In other terms, a peer passes *certain* data to a neighbor. After P collects this data, P uses its DECs to determine its own solutions. This is a recursive definition since the solutions for the neighbors have to be determined first, under the same semantics.

---

[3] In case a peer P trusts itself more than another peer, the information of the latter is irrelevant to P.

Base cases of the recursion are peers with no relevant DECs. As a consequence, this semantics requires an acyclic accessibility graph.

A database instance D of a schema $\mathcal{S}$ can be seen as a finite set of ground facts. If R is a predicate in $\mathcal{S}$, $D|\{R\}$ denotes the extension of R in D. If $\mathcal{R}(\mathsf{P}) \subseteq \mathcal{S}$, $D|\mathsf{P}$ is the restriction of D to $\mathcal{R}(\mathsf{P})$. Below, $\Delta(\cdot, \cdot)$ is used for the symmetric difference of sets.

Definition 1. Given a peer P and instances D, D' on schema $\bigcup_{\mathsf{Q} \in \mathcal{N}(\mathsf{P})} \mathcal{R}(\mathsf{Q})$, D' is a *neighborhood solution for* P *and* D if : (a) $D' \models \bigcup_{\mathsf{Q} \in \mathcal{N}(\mathsf{P})} \Sigma(\mathsf{P}, \mathsf{Q})$. (b) $D'|\{R\} = D|\{R\}$ for every predicate $R \in \mathcal{R}(\mathsf{Q})$ with $(\mathsf{P}, less, \mathsf{Q}) \in trust$. (c) There is no instance D'' satisfying (a), (b), and $\Delta(D, D'') \subsetneqq \Delta(D, D')$. $\qquad\square$

A neighborhood solution for P is a database for its whole neighborhood that satisfies P's DECs and trust relationships. A neighborhood solution stays close to the original instances (and stays the same for trustable peers): The data set that is imported or given up to satisfy the DECs is minimized. $N(\mathsf{P}, D)$ is the set of neighborhood solutions for P, D. The set $S(\mathsf{P})$ of solution instances for P is recursively defined as follows:

Definition 2. For P with local instance $D(\mathsf{P})$, an instance D over $\mathcal{R}(\mathsf{P})$ is a *solution instance* for P if: (a) For $\Sigma(\mathsf{P}) = \emptyset$, $D = D(\mathsf{P})$; (b) For $\Sigma(\mathsf{P}) \neq \emptyset$, $D = \overline{D}|\mathsf{P}$, where $\overline{D} \in N(\mathsf{P}, D(\mathsf{P}) \cup \bigcup_{\mathsf{Q} \in (\mathcal{N}(\mathsf{P}) \smallsetminus \{\mathsf{P}\})} \bigcap_{I \in S(\mathsf{Q})} I)$. $\qquad\square$

Intuitively, before determining P's solutions, P has its local instance $D(\mathsf{P})$, and each neighbor P' has an instance for P that is the intersection of P''s solutions. This produces a combined database $\overline{D}$. Neighborhood solutions for P with $\overline{D}$ can be determined; and their restrictions to P's schema become P's solutions.

The peer consistent answers are the semantically correct answers to a query returned by a peer who consistently considers the data of- and trust relationships with its neighbors.

Definition 3. Let $\mathcal{Q}(\bar{x}) \in \mathcal{L}(\mathsf{P})$ be a FO query. A ground tuple $\bar{t}$ is a *peer consistent* answer (PCA) to $\mathcal{Q}$ from P iff $D \models \mathcal{Q}(\bar{t})$ for every $D \in S(\mathsf{P})$. $\qquad\square$

Example 3 (example 2 continued). The solutions for P1 require the solutions for P2, who needs in its turn the solutions for P3. P3 has no DECs with other peers and its only neighborhood solution is its instance $D(\mathsf{P3})$. This is sent back to P2, who needs to repair $\{R^2(c, 4), R^2(d, 5), S^2(4, 2), S^2(5, 3), R^3(5, 7), R^3(5, 3)\}$ wrt $\Sigma(\mathsf{P2}, \mathsf{P3})$. As P2 trusts P3 the same as itself, it can modify its own data or the data it got from P3. P2 has two neighborhood solutions: $\{R^2(c, 4), R^2(d, 5), S^2(5, 3), R^3(5, 7), R^3(5, 3)\}$ and $\{R^2(c, 4), R^2(d, 5), S^2(4, 2), S^2(5, 3), R^3(5, 7), R^3(5, 3), R^3(4, 2)\}$, that lead to two solutions for P2: $\{R^2(c, 4), R^2(d, 5), S^2(5, 3)\}$ and $\{R^2(c, 4), R^2(d, 5), S^2(4, 2), S^2(5, 3)\}$.

Peer P2 will send to P1 their intersection: $\{R^2(c, 4), R^2(d, 5), S^2(5, 3)\}$. Now, P1 has to repair $\{R^1(c, 4, 2), R^1(f, 3, 5), S^1(3), S^1(7), R^2(c, 4), R^2(d, 5), S^2(5, 3)\}$ wrt $\Sigma(\mathsf{P1}, \mathsf{P2})$. Since P1 trusts P2 more, it will solve inconsistencies by modifying its own data, producing only one neighborhood solution: $\{R^1(c, 4, 2), R^1(f, 3, 5),$

$R^1(d, 5, 3)$, $S^1(3)$, $R^2(c, 4)$, $R^2(d, 5)$, $S^2(5, 3)$}. Thus, $S(\text{P1})$ = {{$R^1(c, 4, 2)$, $R^1(f, 3, 5)$, $R^1(d, 5, 3)$, $S^1(3)$}}.

Similarly, the neighborhood solutions for P4 are {$R^4(5, 3, 3), R^4(5, 7, 3), R^3(5, 7)$, $R^3(5, 3)$} and {$R^4(5, 3, 3), R^3(5, 3)$}. Thus, $S(\text{P4})$ = { {$R^4(5, 3, 3), R^4(5, 7, 3)$}, {$R^4(5, 3, 3)$} }. Thus, if $Q(x, y, z)$: $R^4(x, y, z)$ is posed to P4, its first solution instance returns {⟨5, 3, 3⟩, ⟨5, 7, 3⟩}, and the second, {⟨5, 3, 3⟩}. Then, the only PCA is {⟨5, 3, 3⟩}.   □

In order to answer a query, a peer may not need the whole intersection of solutions for its neighbors, but only the portions of them that are relevant to its DECs and the query at hand. This relevant and certain data can be obtained as PCAs to appropriate queries submitted to its neighbors [3].

3   Answer Set Programs and a Peer's Solutions

Solutions for a peer can be specified as the stable models of disjunctive logic programs (DLPs) [12], also called *answer set programs* [11]. These programs use annotation constants to indicate if an atom has to be virtually inserted or deleted to restore consistency:

Annotation	Atom	The tuple $P(\bar{a})$ is ...
t	$\underline{P}(\bar{a}, \mathbf{t})$	advised to be made true
f	$\underline{P}(\bar{a}, \mathbf{f})$	advised to be made false
t*	$\underline{P}(\bar{a}, \mathbf{t}^\star)$	true or becomes true
t**	$\underline{P}(\bar{a}, \mathbf{t}^{\star\star})$	true in the solution

Here, $\underline{P}$ is a predicate obtained from the database predicate P by adding a new argument to accommodate annotations. Each peer P has a local, facts-free program that depends on its DECs. P, when posed a query, will run it with a query program, using as facts those in its local instance and the relevant ones from the intersections of the solutions of its neighbors. To get the latter, P sends to each neighbor P' queries of the form Q : $R(\bar{x})$, where R is a relation of P' that appears in $\Sigma(\text{P}, \text{P}')$. In order to return to P the PCAs to its queries, the neighboring peers have to run their own programs. As before, they will need PCAs from their own neighbors; etc. This recursion will eventually reach peers that have no DECs, who will offer answers from their original instances to queries by other peers. Now, propagation of PCAs goes backwards until reaching P, and P gets the facts to run its program and obtain the PCAs to the original query.

Example 4 (example 3 continued). If P1 is posed the query $Q_0(x)$: $S^1(x)$, it will need data from the intersection of the solutions of P2, to check the satisfaction of $\Sigma(\text{P1}, \text{P2})$. Thus, it will send to P2 the queries $Q_1(x, y)$: $R^2(x, y)$ and $Q_2(x, y)$: $S^2(x, y)$, expecting for PCAs to them. Now, P2 sends to P3 a single query, $Q_3(x, y)$: $R^3(x, y)$. Since P3 has no DECs, it returns $Q_3 = $ {⟨5, 7⟩, ⟨5, 3⟩}, directly from $D(\text{P3})$. Thus, P2 has the following answer set program:

$S^2_-(x, y, \mathbf{f}) \vee R^3_-(x, y, \mathbf{t}) \leftarrow S^2_-(x, y, \mathbf{t}^\star), not R^3_-(x, y).$
$S^2_-(x, y, \mathbf{f}) \vee R^3_-(x, y, \mathbf{t}) \leftarrow S^2_-(x, y, \mathbf{t}^\star), R^3_-(x, y, \mathbf{f}).$
$R^2_-(x, y, \mathbf{t}^\star) \leftarrow R^2_-(x, y, \mathbf{t}).$
$R^2_-(x, y, \mathbf{t}^\star) \leftarrow R^2(x, y).$ $\left.\begin{array}{l} \\ \\ \\ \\ \end{array}\right\}$ Similarly for
$\leftarrow R^2_-(x, y, \mathbf{t}), R^2_-(x, y, \mathbf{f}).$ S^2 and R^3
$R^2_-(x, y, \mathbf{t}^{\star\star}) \leftarrow R^2_-(x, y, \mathbf{t}^\star), not R^2_-(x, y, \mathbf{f}).$

$R^2(c, 4).\quad R^2(d, 5).\quad S^2(4, 2).\quad S^2(5, 3).\quad R^3(5, 7).\quad R^3(5, 3).$

The facts of this program are those in P2's instance and the PCAs from P3. The first two rules enforce the satisfaction of the DEC $\forall xy\ (S^2(x, y) \to R^3(x, y))$, e.g. the first rule specifies that if $S^2(x, y)$ is true and $R^3(x, y)$ is not in P2's database, then either $S^2(x, y)$ is deleted ($\mathbf{f}$) or $R^3(x, y)$ is inserted ($\mathbf{t}$). The other rules capture the semantics of the annotations. The fifth rule, i.e. the program denial constraint, prevents a database atom from being both inserted and deleted. Atoms annotated with $\mathbf{t}^{\star\star}$ in a stable model of the program correspond to those in the associated solution for P2. Stable models and solutions are in 1-1 correspondence. The program above is run by P2 with the queries posed by P1, e.g. for $\mathcal{Q}_1$ with query rule $Ans_1(x, y) \leftarrow R^2_-(x, y, \mathbf{t}^{\star\star})$. P2 sends to P1 the PCAs $\{\langle c, 4\rangle, \langle d, 5\rangle\}$ for $\mathcal{Q}_1$, and $\{\langle 5, 3\rangle\}$ for $\mathcal{Q}_2$. Now, P1 has all the facts for its program:

$R^1_-(x, y, z, \mathbf{t}) \leftarrow R^2_-(x, y, \mathbf{t}^\star), S^2_-(y, z, \mathbf{t}^\star),\ not\ R^1_-(x, y, z).$
$R^1_-(x, y, z, \mathbf{t}) \leftarrow R^2_-(x, y, \mathbf{t}^\star), S^2_-(y, z, \mathbf{t}^\star), R^1_-(x, y, z, \mathbf{f}).$
$S^1_-(x, \mathbf{f}) \leftarrow S^1_-(x, \mathbf{t}^\star),\ not\ S^2_-(5, x).$
$S^1_-(x, \mathbf{f}) \leftarrow S^1_-(x, \mathbf{t}^\star), S^2_-(5, x, \mathbf{f}).$

$R^2_-(x, y, \mathbf{t}^\star) \leftarrow R^2_-(x, y, \mathbf{t}).$
$R^2_-(x, y, \mathbf{t}^\star) \leftarrow R^2(x, y).$ $\left.\begin{array}{l} \\ \\ \\ \\ \end{array}\right\}$ Similarly for
$\leftarrow R^2_-(x, y, \mathbf{t}), R^2_-(x, y, \mathbf{f}).$ S^2 and R^1
$R^2_-(x, y, \mathbf{t}^{\star\star}) \leftarrow R^2_-(x, y, \mathbf{t}^\star), not R^2_-(x, y, \mathbf{f}).$

$R^1(c, 4, 2).\quad R^1(f, 3, 5).\quad R^1(d, 5, 3).\quad S^1(3).\quad R^2(c, 4).\quad R^2(d, 5).\quad S^2(5, 3).$

The first two rules enforce the satisfaction of the DEC $\forall xyz\ (R^2(x, y) \wedge S^2(y, z) \to R^1(x, y, z))$; and the third and fourth rules, the second DEC $\forall x\ (S^1(x) \to S^2(5, x))$.

Now, P1 is able to peer consistently answer the original query $\mathcal{Q}_0$: $S^1(x)$ by running the query rule $Ans_0(x) \leftarrow S^1_-(x, \mathbf{t}^{\star\star})$ together with the program above that specifies its solutions. The ground Ans_0-atoms in the intersection of all stable models, in this case only $Ans_0(3, \mathbf{t}^{\star\star})$, are the cautions answers from the solution program. They correspond to the PCAs, in this case only $\langle 3 \rangle$. $\square$

4   Discussion

We have illustrated the semantics on the bases of universal DECS. However, the semantics can be extended to DECs that include referential DECs. For example, we could have a peer system with the following sets of DECs:

$$\mathcal{P}_1 : \ \Sigma(\text{P1},\text{P2}) = \{\forall xy \ (R^1(x,y) \to R^2(x,y)), \forall xy \ (R^2(x,y) \to R^1(x,y))\},$$
$$\Sigma(\text{P2},\text{P1}) = \{\forall x(S^2(x) \to \exists y S^1(x,y))\}.$$

In this case, inconsistency wrt the latter DEC can be restored by introducing null values (into the second argument of S^1). A repair semantics based on null values for sets of ICs that include referential ICs was introduced and analyzed in [5]. This semantics can be adapted to the case of DECs in a peer data exchange system [3]. The solutions for a peer can be specified by means of answer set programs. Actually, in the case the DECs are *ref-acyclic*, i.e. without cycles through referential DECs, there is a 1-1 correspondence between solution instances and models of the program. For example, $\mathcal{P}_1$ above is ref-acyclic, whereas the following system $\mathcal{P}_2$ is not: $\Sigma(\text{P1},\text{P2}) = \{\forall xy \ (R^1(x,y) \to \exists z \ R^2(x,z)), \forall xy \ (R^2(x,y) \to R^1(x,y))\}$. Sets of universal DECs are always ref-acyclic.

The problem of deciding peer consistent query answering is Π_2^P-complete in data [3], which matches the complexity of cautious query evaluation from DLPs. However, it is possible to identify syntactic classes of PDESs for which peer consistent query answering has a lower complexity [3]. It is also possible to identify cases in which the requirement of an acyclic accessibility graph can be relaxed [3]. This is the usual *unrestricted import case*, where the DECs are such that data is only imported into the peer (nothing is deleted), and all peers trust other peers more than themselves. In this case, peers always have solution instances, and the solution program can be replaced by a non-disjunctive program. In particular, the problem of determining if a tuple is a peer consistent answer to a query is in *coNP* [3].

It is possible to relax the conditions of ref-acyclicity and acyclicity of the peer graph, still providing a sensible semantics, and correct and complete solution-programs can be given. This is the case when, for example the cycles in the graph are not be relevant to the query. Even if the DECs are not ref-acyclic, depending on the interaction with the trust relationships, the solution program can capture exactly the set of solution instances.

Logic programs can be used to compute solutions for a peer and also PCAs. Techniques to partially compute solution instances can be useful, since we are not interested in them per se, but in the PCAs. In order to reduce the number of rules and the amount of data that are needed to run the combined query and solution program, it is possible to apply certain techniques developed for CQA. Among them we find *magic sets* for stable model semantics, and the identification of predicates that are relevant to queries and constraints [8, 9].

We can handle local ICs for peers, in addition to the DECs a peer may have with other peers. The semantics for peer solution instances can be uniformly and smoothly extended to include these local ICs. The latter will also determine the solutions for a peer, for they have to be satisfied when the local instance is virtually updated due to the presence of other peers [3]. This extension can be obtained by having "local" sets of DECs of the form $\Sigma(\text{P1},\text{P1})$. For example, $\forall xyz(R^1(x,y,z) \to S^1(z)) \in \Sigma(\text{P1},\text{P1}) \subseteq \mathcal{L}(\text{P1})$ could be an integrity constraint on the schema $\mathcal{R}(\text{P1})$ of P1.

For comparison with related work around PDESs, we should mention [10, 7], whose semantics for PDESs have some similarities with ours (but no trust relationships). For example, in [10] DECs are of the form $cq_i \rightarrow cq_j$, where cq_i and cq_j are conjunctive queries over Pi and Pj's schemas, resp. However, their semantics for data exchange is based on *epistemic logic*. There are no trust relationships, but implicitly, peers trust themselves less than other peers. Local ICs violations are avoided by ignoring a peer that is inconsistent wrt its local ICs. New atoms are added into a peer by interaction with other peers only if this does not produce a local IC violation.

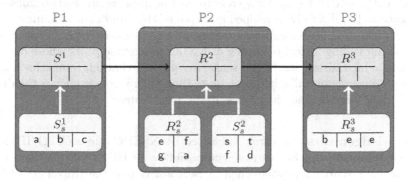

Each peer is considered as a local virtual data integration system with *GAV local mappings* [6], in this case: $\forall xyz(S_s^1(x,y,z) \rightarrow S^1(x,y,z))$, $\forall xyz(R_s^2(x,y) \wedge R_s^2(y,z) \rightarrow R^2(x,y,z))$, $\forall xyz(R_s^3(x,y,z) \rightarrow R^3(x,y,z))$. The predicates of the form P_s correspond to local sources, and those of the form P^i correspond to the mediated schema provided by peer Pi. The DECs establish mapping between the latter. In this case: $\forall xy(R^2(x,y,z) \rightarrow \exists w R^1(x,y,w))$, $\forall xy(R^3(x,y,y) \rightarrow \exists uv R^3(u,x,v))$.

For query answering, the following epistemic theory is used:

$$\left. \begin{array}{l} \mathbf{K_1}(\forall xyz(S_s^1(x,y,z) \rightarrow S^1(x,y,z))) \\ \forall xy(\mathbf{K_2}(R^2(x,y,z)) \rightarrow \mathbf{K_1}(\exists w R^1(x,y,w))) \end{array} \right\} \text{Specification of P1}$$

$$\left. \begin{array}{l} \mathbf{K_2}(\forall xyz(R_s^2(x,y) \wedge R_s^2(y,z) \rightarrow R^2(x,y,z))) \\ \forall xy(\mathbf{K_3}(R^3(x,y,y)) \rightarrow \mathbf{K_2}(\exists uv R^3(u,x,v)))\} \end{array} \right\} \text{Specification of P2}$$

$$\mathbf{K_3}(\forall xyz(R_s^3(x,y,z) \rightarrow R^3(x,y,z))) \qquad \} \text{Specification of P3}$$

$\mathbf{K_i}\phi$ is interpreted as ϕ is known by peer Pi. The idea behind using the epistemic theory is that data that is known (or certain) is passed from local sources to mediated schemas and from peers to other peers. A tuple $\bar{t}$ is a peer consistent answer to a query $\mathcal{Q}$ posed to peer Pi if $\mathbf{K_i}\mathcal{Q}(\bar{t})$ is a logical consequence of the epistemic theory.

An advantage of this approach is that the semantics can be applied in the presence of cycles. However, possibly the whole epistemic theory has to be used by a peer Pi to do query answering, which requires not only data, but also the mappings and DECs; and this not only of its neighbors, but of all accessible peers.

Our approach can be easily and uniformly adapted in order to make each peer a local data integration system. For this, the specifications and answer set programs for virtual data integration introduced in [1] can be used in combination with those presented here.

We emphasize that the DECs we can handle are more general that those found in related work, including mappings between ontologies, which -when the latter are merged- requires addressing the inconsistencies that naturally emerge [13]. In particular, our DECs may have relations of both peers on the two sides of the implication. In [2] a fully developed example of this kind can be found.

Our semantics allows for inconsistent peers and inconsistencies between peers, without unraveling logical reasoning or having to exclude peers whose data participates in inconsistencies. In this sense, we may say that our semantics is *inconsistency tolerant*. Actually, it is even more than this: inconsistency is the driving and guiding force behind the process of data exchange.

Acknowledgements. Research supported by NSERC and a CITO/IBM-CAS Student Internship. L. Bertossi is Faculty Fellow of IBM CAS (Toronto Lab.). Part of this research was done when L. Bertossi visited the University of Edinburgh in 2007. The invitation and hospitality are much appreciated.

References

[1] Bertossi, L., Bravo, L.: Consistent Query Answers in Virtual Data Integration Systems. In: Bertossi, L., Hunter, A., Schaub, T. (eds.) Inconsistency Tolerance. LNCS, vol. 3300, pp. 42–83. Springer, Heidelberg (2004)

[2] Bertossi, L., Bravo, L.: Query Answering in Peer-to-Peer Data Exchange Systems. In: Lindner, W., Mesiti, M., Türker, C., Tzitzikas, Y., Vakali, A.I. (eds.) EDBT 2004. LNCS, vol. 3268, pp. 476–485. Springer, Heidelberg (2004)

[3] Bertossi, L., Bravo, L.: The Semantics of Consistency and Trust in Peer Data Exchange Systems. In: Dershowitz, N., Voronkov, A. (eds.) LPAR 2007. LNCS (LNAI), vol. 4790, pp. 107–122. Springer, Heidelberg (2007)

[4] Bertossi, L.: Consistent Query Answering in Databases. ACM Sigmod Record 2(35), 68–76 (2006)

[5] Bravo, L., Bertossi, L.: Semantically Correct Query Answers in the Presence of Null Values. In: Grust, T., Höpfner, H., Illarramendi, A., Jablonski, S., Mesiti, M., Müller, S., Patranjan, P.-L., Sattler, K.-U., Spiliopoulou, M., Wijsen, J. (eds.) EDBT 2006. LNCS, vol. 4254, pp. 336–357. Springer, Heidelberg (2006)

[6] Lenzerini, M.: Data Integration: A Theoretical Perspective. In: Proc. Symposium on Principles of Database Systems (PODS 2002), pp. 233–246. ACM Press, New York (2002)

[7] Calvanese, D., De Giacomo, G., Lembo, D., Lenzerini, M., Rosati, R.: Inconsistency Tolerance in P2P Data Integration: An Epistemic Logic Approach. In: Bierman, G., Koch, C. (eds.) DBPL 2005. LNCS, vol. 3774, pp. 90–105. Springer, Heidelberg (2005)

[8] Caniupan, M., Bertossi, L.: The Consistency Extractor System: Querying Inconsistent Databases using Answer Set Programs. In: Prade, H., Subrahmanian, V.S. (eds.) SUM 2007. LNCS (LNAI), vol. 4772, pp. 74–88. Springer, Heidelberg (2007)

[9] Eiter, T., Fink, M., Greco, G., Lembo, D.: Efficient Evaluation of Logic Programs for Querying Data Integration Systems. In: Palamidessi, C. (ed.) ICLP 2003. LNCS, vol. 2916, pp. 163–177. Springer, Heidelberg (2003)

[10] Franconi, E., Kuper, G., Lopatenko, A., Zaihrayeu, I.: A Distributed Algorithm for Robust Data Sharing and Updates in P2P Database Networks. In: Lindner, W., Mesiti, M., Türker, C., Tzitzikas, Y., Vakali, A.I. (eds.) EDBT 2004. LNCS, vol. 3268, pp. 446–455. Springer, Heidelberg (2004)

[11] Gelfond, M., Leone, N.: Logic Programming and Knowledge Representation - The A-Prolog Perspective. Artificial Intelligence 138(1-2), 3–38 (2002)

[12] Gelfond, M., Lifschitz, V.: Classical Negation in Logic Programs and Disjunctive Databases. New Generation Computing 9(3/4), 365–386 (1991)

[13] Serafini, L., Borgida, A., Tamilin, A.: Aspects of Distributed and Modular Ontology Reasoning. In: Proc. International Joint Conference on Artificial Intelligence (IJCAI 2005), pp. 570–575. Morgan Kaufmann, San Francisco (2005)

Correlated Query Process and P2P Execution

Qiming Chen and Meichun Hsu

HP Labs
Palo Alto, California, USA
Hewlett Packard Co
{qiming.chen,meichun.hsu}@hp.com

Abstract. A technical trend in supporting data intensive applications is to push-down them to database engines by wrapping computations with User Defined Functions (UDFs) callable from the SQL interface. For seamlessly integrating applications into SQL queries, we introduce a special kind of UDFs with both input and output as relations, or row sets, called Relation Valued Functions (RVFs). As a single SQL statement has limited expressive power on complex data flows and control flows, we propose the notion of *Correlated Query Process* (CQP), for specifying an application at the process level, by several queries and RVFs with interleaved steps.

We further extend this notion to Collaborative CQP with multiple participating parties which have correlated but separate goals. A truly P2P execution model is proposed, under which the logical execution of a collaborative CQP consists of a set of individual peer CQP executions run by the participating parties. These peer executions are based on the same CQP template; but each peer represents a designated role, it actively processes the steps belong to that role, and skip the steps not belonging to that role. They synchronize peer CQP executions by passing the query return messages. This collaborative process execution model represents a shift from coordinator based distributed query processing to truly P2P collaboration.

This work represents an initial step to the synthesis of relational operation, UDF and business process. We further envisage that the proposed P2P CQP execution model will have impact not only on inter-enterprise collaboration but also on the cooperation of multiple share-nothing data servers.

1 Introduction

The Problem. Pushing down analytical computations to database engines can provide many benefits, including the ability to perform entire data analysis directly through the SQL-based interface, reduced data transfer costs between the database and the application, and faster, parallel data access [5,6,8,10]. The major mechanism for this is to wrap applications with User Defined Functions (UDFs) which can be embedded in SQL statements. However, a single SQL statement has limited expressive power at the application level, since the data flow represented in a SQL query is coincident with the control flow, but an application often requires additional data flows between its steps. In the other words, a query tree represents both the data flows and control flows of its steps, but an application is often modeled as a DAG (Directed Acyclic

A. Hameurlain (Ed.): Globe 2008, LNCS 5187, pp. 82–92, 2008.
© Springer-Verlag Berlin Heidelberg 2008

Graph) with separate data flows and control flows between its steps. In order to converge data intensive computation and data management while keeping the *high-level* SQL interface, we envisage the need for the synthesis of relational operation, UDF and business process.

Very often, multiple peer systems must work collaboratively for their correlated goals, since their data sources may be separated, and their data processing capabilities may be different. With the current technologies, distributed query processing and P2P query processing are primarily based on the coordination model, with query result returned to the initial requestor [1,2,14]. In the truly P2P environment, peers such as s buyer and a seller often have correlated but separate goals. In enterprise information mashup, multiple parties with different but correlated goals need to work collaboratively for sharing each others data and computation results [3,4]. Therefore, multi-goal oriented, process-level collaborative information processing is identified as another technical challenge.

Our Solution. We introduce a special kind of UDFs with both input and output as relations, or row sets, called Relation Valued Functions (RVFs), for seamlessly integrating applications into SQL queries. Then we propose the notion of *Correlated Query Process* (CQP), for specifying an application by several queries and RVFs with interleaved steps. In a CQP, a query may stand for a step or be divided into multiple steps where each step represents a data transformation. This approach combines the high-level declarative semantics in the spirit of SQL, and the procedural semantics found in business processes.

We further consider the *Collaborative* CQP with multiple participating peersystems; these peers have correlated but separate goals; each peer is assigned a role, and each step query is the responsibility of a designated role; the executors of step queries are self-selected by the participating peers through role-matching.

Unlike the coordinator based distributed query processing and P2P query processing models, the logical execution of a collaborative CQP consists of a set of individual peer CQP executions run by multiple participating parties, each for its own goal. These peer executions are based on the same CQP template; but each peer represents a designated role, it actively processes the steps belonging to that role, and skips the steps not belonging to that role. The actual executor of a step will forward the return message of query execution to other peers, embedded with the query or RVF results to be visible (selected on the per peer basis), for them to roll forward their own peer process executions.

Comparison with Related Work. We share the spirit of Pig Latin [12] to view a query as a process. However, Pig Latin focuses on a single read-only query without separate data flows and control flows between the query steps. Our approach is characterized by dealing with multiple correlate queries with interleaving steps which really form a process, and by the P2P process execution by multiple parties. Compared with general workflow [4,7,15], our approach can be viewed as the synthesis of relational algebra and business process. A CQP is a light-weight business process made only by query and RVF steps, its collaborative execution is based on synchronizing decentralized, individual peer executions simply through forwarding the query return messages from SQL engines. This is very different from the choreography mechanism found in business process interaction such as specified in BPEL. In the context of distributed query processing, the collaborative CQP execution model is role-based, P2P and non-coordinated. It differs from the distributed query processing [11,13] where a coordinator is responsible for scheduling subquery execution; and differs from most P2P query processing [1,2,9,16] where a query is initiated from a peer, assisted by peers, and having result returned to the initiator. Further a distinguish feature of collaborative CQP is that the participating parties actually have separate goals, through correlated, thus any centralized process execution or coordinated distributed execution may not fit in. Finally, compared with database script languages, we focus on the process-level rather than programming level solution.

This approach realizes the synthesis of relational operation, UDF and business process, which allows analytical computations to be pushed down to database engines and performed through *high-level* SQL interface. The notion of CQP lifts query answering to the process level, and the collaborative CQP execution model represents a shift from the single goal oriented, coordination based distributed query processing to multi-goal oriented, truly P2P collaboration. The feasibility of this approach has been demonstrated by our prototype.

The rest of this paper is organized as follows: Section 2 introduces the notion of CQP; Section 3 describes collaborative CQP; Section 4 proposes the P2P collaborative CQP execution model; Section 5 discusses implementation issues; Section 6 concludes.

2   Correlated Query Process

A SQL statement expresses the composition of several data access and manipulation functions. A query execution plan can be viewed as a process including sequential and parallel steps, which opens the potential of handling queries at the process level.

For example, Pig Latin developed at Yahoo Research combines the high-level declarative querying in the spirit of SQL, and low-level, procedural programming `a la map-reduce [12]. An Example given in [12] shows that given a table urls: (url, category, page-rank), a SQL query that finds, for each sufficiently large category, the average page-rank of high page-rank urls

```
SELECT category, AVG(pagerank) FROM urls
    WHERE pagerank>0.2 GROUP BY category HAVING COUNT(*)>1000000
```

can be expressed as the following "Pig Latin program"

```
good urls = FILTER urls BY pagerank > 0.2;
groups = GROUP good urls BY category;
big groups = FILTER groups BY COUNT(good urls)>1000000;
output = FOREACH big groups GENERATE
category, AVG(good urls.pagerank);
```

that is a sequence of steps, each of which carries out a single data transformation. In fact, a Pig Latin program looks similar to a query execution plan, or a data-flow graph.

We share the same view as Pig Latin in treating a query as a process; however, beyond such a view, we have our specific research goals.

- As a database centric solution, we specify "steps" as individual SQL queries to be optimized by the underlying database engines. For modeling complex applications, we consider multiple correlated queries together with complex data flows and control flows represented as a DAG other than a single query tree.
- Most significantly, we consider a P2P collaborative process execution model.

2.1 RVF – Embedding Data Intensive Computations to SQL Query

UDFs provide a way for introducing computations to SQL. Currently UDFs can be categorized as scalar UDFs, aggregate UDFs, and table UDFs. A table UDF, also called Table Valued Function (TVF), returns a table. In order to handle applications in the SQL framework smoothly, we introduce the kind of UDFs with both input and output as relations, called Relation Valued Functions (RVFs). By definition, an RVF is a function that takes a list of relations, or row sets, as input, and returns a relation, or row set, as its execution result. For instance, a RVF is defined as

CREATE FUNCTION f (t1 TABLE T1, t2 TABLE T2) RETURN T3

where the schemas for T1, T2 and T3 are defined. Note the instance of T1 and T2 can be materialized rows or dynamic query results.

RVF and Query. An RVF performs a relational transformation (although it can have database update effects in the function body), thus can be easily composed in a SQL query. This is because a row-set can be fed in an RVF, and its resulting row-set can be fed in other relation operations naturally, such as

SELECT alert FROM (allert_rvf(SELECT * FROM rivers WHERE water_level >...));

In fact, a query can be viewed as a RVF; reversely, a RVF can be viewed as a query.

Convert UDF to RVF. To convert a UDF to a RVF needs to wrap its input and out put to relations. The handling of output is straightforward. We provided the following two mechanisms to turn input parameters (i.e. argv[]) to a relation.

For converting a list of arguments to a row set, a "system" TVF, a2r is provided that maps a CSV (comma-separated values) to a "system row-set", *args*, as the input of a RVF. For instance, an RVF for eq-joining row sets R, S on attributes $R.A$ and $S.B$ can be expressed as

eq-join (*a2r*("*R.A, S.B*"), *R, S*).

For converting the input of a per-tuple processing UDF to a relation, we can use CROSS APPLY introduced to T-SQL. CROSS APPLY a TVF to a table (or row-set) applies the TVF to each row of the table, unions the resulting row sets, and joins the input table. In the following example, TVF, f (river_seg_id), is applied to the selected set of river segments, resulting in a row set

SELECT * FROM river_segs WHERE river_name = "Red_River"
        CROSS APPLY f (river_seg_id);

Therefore, cross apply a TVF to a row set, can be viewed as a RVF.

2.2 Correlated Query Process with RVF

We represent an application at the process level by one or more correlated SQL queries and RVFs which form the sequential or concurrent steps of that application with
complex data flows between them. Each step is an individual query or RVF that results in a row set.

In a regular query, the data flow and control flow are consistent and represented by
a query tree. Even if with nested structure, a single query is unable to represent a
general DAG-like data flow and control flow. Correlating multiple queries (including
RVFs) into a process allows us to express control flows separately from data flows.

Refer to Figure 1, for instance, an application is modeled as a query Q, followed by
RVF f that takes Q's results as input, then followed by RVFs g_1 and g_2 which take f's
as well as Q's results as input. The data flows and control flows of this application are
not coincident. In order to express data flows separately from control flows, and to
ensure the involved query Q and RVF f to be executed only once, this application
cannot be expressed by a single SQL statement, but by a list of correlated queries at
the process level. Conceptually the data dependency in the above example can be
expressed as a sequence $<Q, f, g_1, g_2>$ meaning that Q should be provided before f,
…etc; this data dependency sequence is not unique ($<Q, f, g_2, g_1>$ is another one) but
correct. The control flow can be expressed by $[Q, f, [g_1, g_2]]$ where $[g_1, g_2]$ can be
executed in parallel.

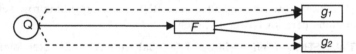

Fig. 1. A simple correlated query process, where data flows (solid and dash lines) and control
flows (solid lines only) are not all coincident

Generally, a *Correlated Query Process* (*CQP*) is made of one or more correlated
SQL queries, referred to as *query steps*, which may be sequential, concurrent or
nested (for simplicity we omit certain details such as conditional branch). A query
step can be an RVF or a query containing RVFs (other UDFs are not excluded). A
CQP represents a data intensive application at the process level where data flows are
allowed to be separated from control flows, and multiple start and exit points are
allowed. We will give a CQP specification example in the next section.

3 Collaborative CQP

As mentioned earlier, applications like enterprise mashups often require evaluating
correlated queries collaboratively with peers for sharing data and computation capabilities mutually. Motivated by meeting such a requirement, we introduce P2P
collaborative CQP with multiple peer participants.

Commonly Agreed CQP Template. A collaborative CQP is defined as a template
commonly agreed by the participating parties, each having a specific goal, but their

goals are correlated and they need each other's effort to reach these goals. The template includes multiple sequential or parallel steps; each can be accomplished by a SQL query where RVFs may be invoked for embedding application level computations. The output of a step query is named which can be specified as the input of another step.

Role Based Collaboration. A collaborative CQP has a list of *process-roles*, indicating the logical participants. A step query has a *step-role*, and that must match one of the process-roles. For example, given process roles A and B, a step query can have role A or B. For simplicity, in this paper we do not explicitly address the situation where a single role is played by multiple players.

The execution of a collaborative CQP involves multiple concurrent peer executions, where each peer is responsible for the step queries matching its role, and they synchronize through messaging. This is very different from the current execution models found in distributed query processing.

Visibility of Query Results. In a P2P CQP execution, each peer can keep some of the query results or RVF results private. For this we introduce the role based *sharing scope* of a step query. The result of a step query may be *public*, i.e. sharable by all process-roles or role specific. A role-specific result is visible only to the peers assigned the given roles (one or more). By default a local result is always visible to the local peer.

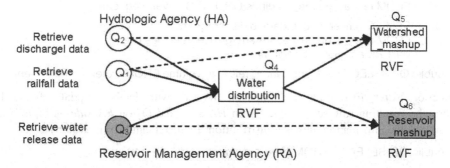

Fig. 2. CQP Co-Mashup has roles HA and RA; the shaded query and RVF are assigned to RA, others are assigned to HA (solid lines for control flows, solid and dash lines for data flows)

Let us consider a collaborative mashup example by the following two organizations.

- A Hydrologic Agency (HA) responsible for water drainage network monitoring.
- A Reservoir Management Agency (RA) responsible for reservoir related operation such as release water for being used by agricultural, industrial, household, etc.

They collaborate on retrieving, processing and integrating information, for generating individually targeted mashup datasets. A mashup dataset is stored in a table with fields for GML (Graphic Mark Language) expressing "feature objects", layout information, urls to external Web pages such as NASA's satellite images, etc, to be fed in a mashup engine for generating a presentation level display. Each organization has its own goal of mashup, but they rely on each others data and scientific computation capabilities to accomplish the mashups. Such collaboration has to be carried out at the process level. A much simplified scenario is shown in Figure 2 and outlined below.

– HA computes the water volume and water level distribution based on rainfall, discharge, evaporation. To generate a mashup for its own goal, it also needs water release data from RA.
– RA generates a separate mashup on its own purpose, based on the above computation results, the reservoir water management related information, as well as other data from Web. As such it relies on the data and computation results from HA.

Involved in this scenario, tables in HA's database, *hadb*, include

– *river_segments* table for static river segment data,
– *rainfall_guage_readings* table for incoming water to river segments,
– *stream_guage_readings* table for outgoing water from river segments.

tables in RA's database, *radb*, include

– *water_management* table for water release and other water management data.

Consider the following simplified queries, Q_1, Q_2 on *HA side* and Q_3 on *RA side*, as well as the UDFs that return tables or row sets.

– Q_1:   SELECT river_seg, date, SUM(rainfall)
         FROM rainfall_guage_readings GROUP BY river_seg, date
– Q_2:   SELECT a.river_seg, b.date, b.discharge_rate
         FROM river_segments a, stream_guage_readings b
         WHERE a.region = b.region
– public Q_3: SELECT river_seg, water_release_volume FROM water_management

Function *Water_distribution* is defined on HA side with database update effects. It takes the resulting row sets of Q_1, Q_2 on *HA side* and Q_3 on *RA side* as input and computes the information on water distribution. Its result can be retrieved by

– public Q_4: SELECT * FROM *Water_distribution* (Q_1, Q_2, Q_3)

Function *Watershed_mashup* is defined on HA side that takes the results of Q_1, Q_2 and RVF *Water_distribution* as input, retrieves satellite images from Web, and generates data to be mashed up for HA. Its result is expressed by

– Q_5:   SELECT * FROM *Watershed_mashup* (Q_1, Q_2, Q_4)

Function *Reservoir_mashup* is defined on RA side, that takes the results of Q_3 and RVF *Water_distribution* as input, retrieves data from Web, and generates data to be mashed up for RA. Its result can be retrieved by

– Q_6:   SELECT * FROM *Reservoir_mashup* (Q_3, Q_4)

Queries Q_5 and Q_6 represent the ultimate information need for HA and RA.

– They are correlated as they need each other's query or computation results during the processing.

- They cannot be processed individually as function *Water_distribution* has database update effects therefore cannot be executed more than once.
- Thus Q_5 and Q_6 are to be processed interactively with additional data flows to control flows. Instead by query trees, this CQP is represented by a DAG, and Q_5 and Q_6 are actually evaluated at the *process* level.

The CQP process for the above example is specified as below.

```
CREATE QUERY PROCESS co_mashup (
    ROLES HA, RA;
    QUERY STEPS (   //data flow, step role
        Q₁ BY HA: SELECT river_seg, date, SUM(rainfall)
                FROM rainfall_guage_readings GROUP BY river_seg, date;
        Q₂ BY HA: SELECT a.river_seg, b.date, b.discharge_rate
                FROM river_segments a, stream_guage_readings b
                WHERE a.region = b.region;
        public Q₃ BY RA: SELECT river_seg, water_release_volume
                FROM water_management;
        public Q₄ BY HA: SELECT * FROM Water_distribution (Q1, Q2, Q3);
        Q₅ BY HA: SELECT * FROM Watershed_mashup (Q1, Q2, Q4);
        Q₆ BY RA: SELECT * FROM Reservoir_mashup (Q3, Q4);
    )
    SEQUENCE (   //control flow, concurrency
        [Q₁, Q₂, Q₃], Q₄, [Q₅, Q₆];
    )
)
```

In summary, a collaborative CQP expresses the collaboration of multiple peers with specific but correlated goals at the query process level.

4 A P2P CQP Execution Model

In this section we will discuss a truly P2P execution model of collaborative CQPs. Unlike the coordinator based distributed query processing and P2P query processing models, the logical execution of a collaborative CQP consists of a set of individual peer CQP executions run by the participating parties. These peer executions are based on the same CQP template; but each peer represents a designated role, it actively executes the steps belong to that role, and skips (passive executes) the steps not belonging to that role.

The actual executor of a step query gets a return message, *rmsg*, from the local database engine, containing the execution status and resulting data. It simply forwards this *rmsg* to the participating peers for synchronizing the executions of their peer processes, while for each peer, it encloses in the forwarded *rmsg* only the query re-sults visible to it. The local process execution rolls forward to the next step upon receipt of *rmsg* from the current step execution, the peer process executions also roll forward to the next step upon receipt of the forwarded *rmsg*.

For any peer, if a step query does not belong to its role thus is skipped by it, as a *passive step*, no *rmsg* is returned; instead, this peer waits for the forwarded *rmsg* to move to the next step.

At minimum, a *rmsg* contains the following information:

- global execution ID of the logical CQP execution,
- local IDs of the peer CQP execution and the step query execution,
- step query execution status,
- the resulting row set (may not forwarded to all peers)

In summary, when a collaborative CQP is *defined*, it is specified with the process-roles and step-roles. When a logical execution is *created*, the players (peers) and the roles they play are specified. The system at the creating party obtains a global execution ID for this logical execution, creates a peer execution for itself, and associates this ID with its peer execution. When the system at the creating party sends requests to other peers (i.e., the other players of the CQP) to *instantiate* the peer executions, the global execution ID is also specified. This global execution ID is encapsulated in all the messages on the above logical execution, and transferred to all peer sides to correlate peer executions of the collaborative CQP execution. During the process execution,

- the step queries are "processed" at all the peer executions; however, for a specific step query, if the peer role matches its step role, it will be *actively executed*, otherwise it will be *skipped*;
- after each active execution of a step query, a status massage is returned to the execution site, and propagated to all the other participating sites for synchronize the peer executions - upon receipt of this message, all the peer executions roll forward to the next step;
- step query results are exchanged with the above return message according to the visibility of peer roles to the data.

The Co-Mashup CQP illustrated by Figure 2 of last Section is executed by peers HA and RA collaboratively in the following way:

- HA and RA honor the same CQP template but each side has its own a peer instance, and a designated role for the execution. Shown in Figure 3, the steps belong to the corresponding role are shaded.
- A peer CQP execution is initiated at HA side, representing the process-role of HA, and through messaging, HB is told to create a counterpart peer execution.
- Based on role-matching, HA actively executes step queries Q_1, Q_2 and skips Q_3; RA actively executes Q_3 and skips Q_1 and Q_2. The *rmsgs* from each step execution is forwarded to the other player of the process, for it to update their peer process state and schedule the possible next step of their own peer execution.
- The peer CQP executions at both sides carry out step by step in this way, towards their ends.

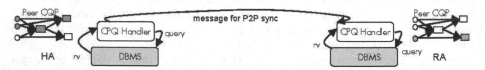

Fig. 3. P2P CQP execution has multiple peer execution instances; which honor the common CQP template but each is responsible for the steps matching its role (shaded)

5 Implementation Issues

We have implemented the CQP handler on top of Oracle DBMS with JDBC interface. This novel integration achieves two purposes: on the one hand, it provides a platform for demonstrate the non-coordination based, truly P2P data processing model; on the other hand, it elevates UDF based data intensive applications from query level to collaborative process level.

The CQP handler is provided with activity scheduling capability based on the usual graph based process model. An activity is simply a query or RVF invocation. A query is dispatched to the underlying database. Currently we limit RVFs to those equivalent to R CROSS APPLY f() where R is a table and f is a tuple oriented UDF for them to be push-down to certain database engines (e.g. SQL Server, My Sql).

The CQP handlers then become the communicator of the participating DBMSs. Their properties relating to such communications such as domain names, local names and protocol, must be visible to peers. In addition, when executing a CQP a *logical identifier*, global execution ID, for the execution must be obtained, that is used to identify a logical instance of execution for correlating and synchronizing the multiple peer executions. All the messages exchanged for that execution are marked by that unique global execution ID. This is necessary to distinguish the multiple concurrent peer executions run by a CQP handler. Each CQP handler maintains a mapping table between the global ID and the local ID for each CQP execution. When a message relating to the execution of a CQP is received, the global execution ID is used to identify the corresponding local execution.

The CQP handler is treated as a virtual database layer in the following sense. It relies on the underlying database to store intermediate results (e.g. in terms of temporary tables); it also relies on the operational environment of the underlying databases for authorization, cache management, garbage collection, etc. In fact, most of the functions at this CQP handler layer can be directly implemented using UDFs.

6 Conclusions

We have presented our solution on P2P collaborative data intensive computation in SQL. We introduced a special kind of UDFs, RVFs, for seamlessly integrating applications into SQL queries. As a single SQL statement has limited expressive power at the application level, we proposed the notion of CQP for composing multiple correlated SQL queries to a process with complex data flows and control flows, which allows pushing-down applications to data management layer effectively.

Further, we have introduced the notion of role-based collaborative CQP, and proposed a novel CQP collaboration model characterized by P2P synchronization of individual process executions, rather than relying on a coordinator as found in most distributed query processing and grid query processing. This approach has all the advantages of P2P computing. Most significantly, the inter-peer synchronization is so simple, only based on passing the return message of query executions. The feasibility of this approach has been demonstrated by our prototype.

Through this work, we have made conceptual as well as practical contributions to extending SQL framework for converging data intensive computation and data management; in lifting query answering to the process level, and in multi-goals based, truly P2P collaborative information processing. We also envisage the impact of this approach on the cooperation of multiple database systems or a parallel database system with share-nothing data servers, which is worth further investigation.

References

1. Aberer, K., Hauswirth, M.: P2P Information Systems: Concepts and Models, State of the Art, and Future Systems. In: ICDE 2002. 187– Advanced Technology Seminar (2002)
2. Bernstein, P.A., Giunchiglia, F., Kementsietsidis, A., Mylopoulos, J., Serafini, L., Zaihrayeu, I.: Data Management for Peer-to-Peer Computing: A Vision. In: Proc. of WebDB 2002 (2002)
3. Chen, Q., Hsu, M.: CPM Revisited – An Architecture Comparison. In: Proc. of 10th Int'l Conf on Cooperative Information Systems (Coopis 2002), USA (2002)
4. Chen, Q., Hsu, M.: Inter-Enterprise Collaborative Business Process Management. In: Proc. of 17th Int'l Conf on Data Engineering (ICDE 2001), Germany (2001)
5. Chen, Q., Kambayashi, Y.: Nested Relation Based Database Knowledge Representation. In: Proc. of ACM SIGMOD 1991. ACM SIGMOD Rec., vol. 20(2) (1991)
6. Chen, Q.: A Rule-based Object/Task Modeling Approach. In: ACM SIGMOD (1986)
7. Dayal, U., Chen, Q.: From Database Programming to Process Management Programming. In: DBPL-5 (1996)
8. Jim Gray, D.T., Liu, M., Nieto-Santisteban, M.A., Szalay, A.S., Heber, G., DeWitt, D.: Scientific Data Management in the Coming Decade. SIGMOD Record 34(4) (2005)
9. Gribble, S.D., Halevy, A.Y., Ives, Z.G., Rodrig, M., Suciu, D.: What Can Database Do for Peer-to-Peer? In: WebDB 2001, pp. 31–36 (2001)
10. Hsu, M., Xiong, Y.: Building a Scalable Web Query System. In: Bhalla, S. (ed.) DNIS 2007. LNCS, vol. 4777. Springer, Heidelberg (2007)
11. Kossmann, D.: The State of the Art in Distributed Query Processing. ACM Computing Surveys 32, 422–469 (2000)
12. Olston, C., Reed, B., Srivastava, U., Kumar, R., Tomkins, A.: Pig Latin: A Not-So-Foreign Language for Data Processing. In: ACM SIGMOD (2008)
13. Papadimos, V., Maier, D.: Distributed Queries without Distributed State. In: WebDB (2002)
14. Tatarinov, I., Ives, Z., Madhavan, J., Halevy, A., Suciu, D., Dalvi, N., Dong, X.L., Kadiyska, Y., Miklau, G., Mork, P.: The Piazza peer data management project. In: ACM SIGMOD (2003)
15. Workflow Management Coalition, http://www.aiim.org/wfmc/mainframe.htm
16. Yang, B., Garcia-Molina, H.: Comparing Hybrid Peer-to-Peer Systems. In: VLDB 2001 (2001)

Multi-set DHT for Range Queries on Dynamic Data for Grid Information Service*

Georges Da Costa[1], Salvatore Orlando[2], and Marios D. Dikaiakos[3]

[1] IRIT - Universite Paul Sabatier, Toulouse III, France
[2] Department of Computer Science, Ca' Foscari University of Venice, Italy
[3] Department of Computer Science, University of Cyprus, 1678 Nicosia, Cyprus

Abstract. Scalability is a fundamental problem for information systems when the amount of managed data increases. Peer to Peer systems are usually used to solve scalability problems as centralized approaches do not scale without large dedicated infrastructure. But most current Peer to Peer systems do not take into account that indexed data can be dynamic. Thus, we propose the *Multi-set* approach, which aims to find the best trade-off between DHT-based network and total replication. This approach is built over classical DHT Peer to Peer system. It can improve most of pure DHT Peer to Peer system by taking into account the dynamism of indexed data. Evaluation is done by modeling, simulation and experimentation on PlanetLab. The use case is an information service for Grid, where resource attributes are indexed.

1 Introduction

Grids are based on several basic but nevertheless necessary services. One of such services is the information service which manage resources. This service has to keep track of the Grid state and to locate resources corresponding to user queries. Attributes associated with the diverse physical resources making up the Grid can be of various types. They can be static, such as the type of network card, or dynamic, such as network bandwidth. Some attributes can be characterized by an intermediate dynamism, such as the number of free processors in a cluster.

Information service have thus to track the various Grid elements and characteristics. To this end, they have to manage large amounts of distributed and changing information. Information service have to answer to queries which are initiated by users willing to run their applications on the Grid. Moreover, such a system should be able to efficiently answer queries [12] such as: *find clusters with at least 32 free processors and ATM network*.

Difficulties arise due to the large scale of current Grids. Centralized approach shows its limits, since it sacrifices data freshness for efficiency. For example, a system using a tree structure (like the predominant *Monitoring and Discovery System* of Globus) has to increase timeouts to prevent overload of the root [2].

---

* This work was funded by Ercim at CNR-ISTI (Pisa, Italy) and at UCY (Nicosia, Cyprus). This research work is carried out under the FP6 Network of Excellence CoreGRID funded by the European Commission (Contract IST-2002-004265).

A. Hameurlain (Ed.): Globe 2008, LNCS 5187, pp. 93–104, 2008.

Peer to Peer systems are known [9] for having solved the file-sharing scalability problem and for being fault-tolerant and easy to deploy and manage. However, classical Peer to Peer systems (Chord, Freenet) cannot directly be used to solve the problem of Grid information service, as they lack key functionalities, like the ability to give several answers for one query or to answer complex queries.

Peer to Peer systems for Grid information services have been already introduced [1,4]. Even links between databases and Peer to Peer have been explored [6]. However, most of these systems are not yet efficient enough for our purposes: they are not reactive, and in some cases, use a number of communications proportional to the number of clusters in the system. Secondly, most of these studies do not take into account the variability of stored information.

Our goal is to improve current systems [1,4] using a Peer to Peer approach to provide dynamism aware information service. Users ask about particular resources such as: *Where can I find computers with ATM network*, or range of resources such as: *Where can I find storage with at least 1Tb free* or mix of these. Queries are often kept simple because the most versatile the query is, the less optimizations are possible. For this reason, resource attributes in Grids are usually represented as (or can be transformed in) integer numbers. Thus queries submitted by users can be easily translated[4] into logical expression of simple queries about particular resources or range ones. The Grid information service can process those simple queries independently and then merge the results. This model of queries is quite generic as it is possible to translate basic LDAP or XPath queries (used by Globus) into this model. Thus a Grid information service can be built using a simple module that answers range queries, possibly implemented as a distributed service. This basic module shall share the qualities of the whole system: managing dynamic data, answering fully distributed queries and updates, and being scalable. Our proposal of such a system is the *Multi-set DHT* which is optimized for all types of information dynamism.

In the following, we will first evaluate the performance of other systems, then we will present our Multi-set approach, and finally we will evaluate its performance.

2   Related Works on Range Queries

2.1   Context

In the following we will concentrate on the problem of solving range queries and updates on a single resource attribute. The way of managing more complex queries using such basic component can be found in [4].

To this end, we consider a distributed index for each attribute which manages a distributed store of attribute values (*keys*) and pointers to grid nodes (*object*) that provide access to corresponding resources. Assumptions on the objects are: Each object is associated with exactly one key. Keys may change over time. Each query can be either for one key, or for a range of keys. Each key can be associated with any number of objects. For example, for the *Free Processors* attribute, the key 32 is associated with all the clusters that have exactly 32 free processors.

In such a system, the main functionalities are to update the key associated with a value, and to find the object associated with a particular value or a range of values.

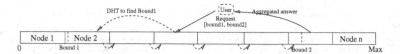

Fig. 1. Key space is split in ranges, one for each peers. To find a range, one has to search for the peer responsible for the range's lower bound, using the global DHT. Then this peer contacts its neighbor, and so on until the upper bound of the range is reached.

Such system needs to react fast to changes to prevent from giving false information users. Moreover such a system must manage peers (nodes that participate in the system) that come and go, due to crashes or simply to local changes of policy.

2.2 Distributed Hash Table (DHT)

DHT Peer to Peer networks are distributed indexes that link integer keys with single objects. Most DHTs efficiently answer simple queries like: locate the peer which could answer a query on a particular key. Typically, the worst case cost to locate an object, in terms of number of messages, is logarithmic with the number of peers. For example, Chord [11] guarantees queries need less than $log(participants)$ messages. Classical Peer to Peer systems are too limited to be directly used for resource management. First, they can only link one object to each key. Secondly they can only answer queries about one single key.

Some systems are using a Peer to Peer approach to address the range query problem: for instance Probe [10], Baton [7], and others [8,5] described in [12]. These systems use the range technique (Figure 1) to provide range functionality.

The query cost of those systems is linear in the size of the range. Keys are spread amongst all the peers, so the larger range is, the more peers it involves. The second query problem is related to the workload distribution as, for some attributes one of the two bounds is always open. For example, queries for the attribute *number of free processors*, users typically ask for clusters with *at least* a certain number of free processors. For *open* range queries, the peer responsible for one of the two extremities of the key space has to answer all the queries. Using one DHT appears to be efficient only when most of requests are updates.

2.3 Other Methods

Another extreme method would be to maintain a total replication of all the objects to be indexed amongst the peers. Queries are free in terms of messages exchanged as they can be processed locally. But changes of resource attributes become very expensive since all peers must be contacted to update their index. This method is suitable when queries largely outnumber updates as cost for updates is linear, and query cost is constant.

3   Mutli-set Approach

In this section we discuss our proposal to manage objects of dynamic characteristics. In the case of a Grid information service, the number of free processors in each site is

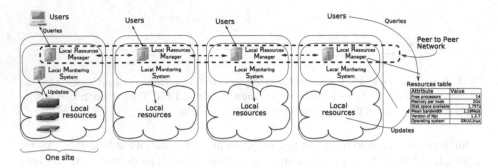

Fig. 2. Each site uses at least one Local Resource Manager (such as GRAM). This *lrm* receives updates concerning the resources it manages locally. It receives queries from users too. When put together in a Peer to Peer network, they forward queries and updates according to local algorithms.

dynamic. In this example, *object* is the site URI[1], and *characteristic* is the number of free processors of the site.

Our Multi-set DHT can be thought as a system that aims to find the best trade-off between the two opposite approaches discussed earlier: the single DHT-based Peer to Peer network that spans across all peers of a Grid system, and the case where the resource index is fully replicated to all Grid peers.

Grid information service is based on information made available by each resource. In the following we consider that *peer*s are the computers that manage the local resources of the Grid sites. Usually, each cluster of the Grid uses a local resource manager such as GRAM in Globus. This allows us to obtain a fully decentralized system. Each user is connected to one of these peers. As a simplification we will only consider the site, the user, and the peer he uses as a single entity. A diagram of this structure is shown in Figure 2.

We will use the term *request* for either update or query. We assume that each resource attribute has its own *ratio of update/request*. As seen in the previous section, classical DHT and total replication are efficient for only a few ratios (when queries are open ones): Total replication is efficient for ratios close to 0 and one DHT for ratios close to 1.

The goal of our Multi-set DHT approach is to provide a transparent system that is able to achieve the best performance possible whatever the ratio is, event if the ratio evolves. To this end, we synchronize several classical DHT, each supported by a distinct *set* of peers. Each peer is in one single *set*, and all *set*s are approximately of the same number of peers.

3.1 Sets

Sets are disjoints groups of peers (Figure 3). Sets are a partition of all the peers. Each of these sets behaves like an range-enabled object management system. All these sets manage the same information. Thus all pairs (*key*, objects), where key is <attribute,

---

[1] *Universal Resource Identifier*, used to contact a site.

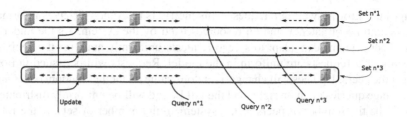

Fig. 3. Multi-set system: Objects are replicated across several groups of peers called *sets*. An *Update* is forwarded to all the sets. A *Query* goes to a random set. The number of sets depends on the ratio Query/Update.

value>, and objects are the list of all Grid resources r which r.attribute = value holds, are duplicated on each set. With this property, a query returns the same value, independently of the chosen set. In order to synchronize the sets, updates are done on each of them. To this end, at any time, each peer keeps at least a reference to a random peer of each set. When an update is issued on a peer, it is processed locally on the set and, at the same time, it is sent to the other sets to keep them up-to-date. To distribute evenly the workload on all the peers, these references are used for queries too. When a query is issued on a peer, the peer chooses randomly a set to process it. In the following, sets are implemented as range enabled DHT systems.

The two fundamental operations provided (Figure 3) are:

Update: In this system, an update is done by contacting an element of each set and using the usual update system of the set.

Query: A query is done by first querying a peer of a randomly chosen set and then using the usual query system of the set.

Intuitively, the update cost increases with the number of sets as there are more sets to inform of the change. In contrast, the query cost decreases as the query is solved inside one set, and the size of each set is reduced when the number of sets grows.

3.2 Trade-Off

Multi-set DHT with one set corresponds to *a single DHT* case, whereas one peer per set corresponds to the total replication case.

The Multi-set approach lies between those two extremes. As the ratio Update/Requests evolves over the time, it adapts *update* and *query* costs depending on its use. With this system, *Updates* become more costly as the number of sets increases, but *Queries* become less expensive. By adapting the number of sets to the ratio Query/Update, a good trade-off can be achieved. Coordinators obtain information from peers to deduce the current ratio. Then they adapt the number of sets by using two methods: Merging, which decreases the number of sets, and Splitting, which creates a new set.

3.3 Model

A first step to evaluate the quality of this approach is to model it and compare to the other two extremes approaches. To compare them, metrics will be the mean number of messages used for answering a request. This metric is relevant as it gives information at the same time on latency and on resources used by the system. As the underlying Peer to Peer systems can adapt to spread requests uniformly amongst the peers [13], we assume that requests are uniform in the model. Requests will be issued uniformly amongst the peers. Updates will change a random value to another random one. Queries will be range queries open on right, and the left bound will be uniformly distributed.

Let N be the number of peers in the system, p the number of sets, α the ratio of updates. The probability that a generic request is an update is α, while the probability that it is a query is $1 - \alpha$. Peers are supposed to be uniformly distributed amongst the key space. We use the chord underlying systems which uses $\ln n$ messages on average in a n peers system to locate an object using its key [11].

Update cost for one DHT: Two operations are done, first remove the old value, then insert the new one. The cost is thus: $2 \ln N$.

Query cost for one DHT: As peers are uniformly distributed, the cost for one query is proportional to the size of the range. The mean size of the range is half the key space. To answer a query regarding half the key space, half the peers needs to be contacted. The cost of contacting the first bound is $\ln N$. The cost is thus: $\frac{N}{2} + \ln N$.

Query cost for total replication: No communication as all objects are stored locally.

Query cost for total replication: All peers are updated: $N - 1$ communications.

Update cost for p sets: Update is done on the current set (of $\frac{N}{p}$ peers), then on the others ones. Beside the real updates, $p - 1$ communications to contact the other sets are needed. Finally the cost is: $2p \ln(\frac{N}{p}) + (p - 1)$.

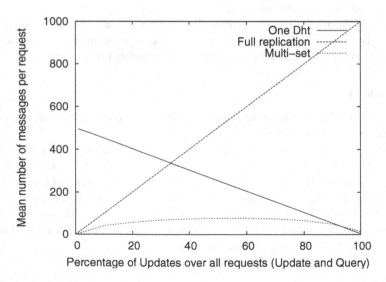

Fig. 4. Model of the mean number of messages for a request depending on the ration Update/Requests. The two classical approaches are shown as a comparison. This system is composed of 1000 peers. p is chosen for each point of the Multi-set curve to minimize the mean cost.

Query cost for p sets: There is only one set that answers the query. There is a probability of $\frac{1}{p}$ to randomly choose the local set and thus to prevent one communication between the sets. The cost is: $\frac{p-1}{p} + \frac{N}{2p}$.

Request cost for p sets: Consequently the mean cost of a request in the Multi-set system is: $\alpha * (2p \ln(\frac{N}{p}) + (p - 1)) + (1 - \alpha)(\frac{p-1}{p} + \frac{N}{2p})$.

This function has only one minimum with $p > 0$.

The curves on figure 4 show the three costs. For each α, the p used for the Multi-set is the one that minimizes the mean cost.

3.4 Algorithms

For each ratio there exists an optimal number of sets that minimizes the number of messages in the system. This number depends on the number of peers too.

As those values evolve over time, it is not possible to define them once and for all before launching the Multi-set. Thus it must be able to evolve towards the optimal number of sets when running. To achieve this we needs first to evaluate the right number of sets, and then to be able to change it.

The three basic operations on which this system is based are the following:

Decision. Which chooses when to do a *Merge* or a *Split*.
Merge. Which reduces the number of sets by one.
Split. Which increases the number of sets by one.

Except during a split, all peers know at least one peer of each other sets. Decisions do not occur frequently beyond initialization as patterns of use do not often change. For the following operations, each set has a peer responsible for all the set, called *supervisor*. In the case of Chord, the supervisor is the one that manages key 0. Each set has a identifier. In this description, for p sets, the identifiers will be $1..p$. Pseudo-code for those algorithms can be found in [3].

Decision Process. The right number of sets is decided by the supervisor. Each supervisor can initiate a change (increase or decrease) in the number of sets.

Supervisors need to evaluate the current ratio of Update/Request in the system. To this end, all peers send regularly the number and type of requests they received to their supervisor. Each supervisor uses those information sent by peers of its set and extracts an evaluation of the ratio from them. Using this estimated ratio and an estimation of the number of peers, the supervisor uses the model to evaluate the optimal number of set according to the environment. If a change is necessary, one supervisor notifies the others that a *Merge* or a *Split* is scheduled and initiates it.

Merge. It is based on the capability of the underlying DHT systems to support peers that dynamically join/leave the system.

When a merge is decided, one set is chosen to be destroyed. Then the supervisor for this set asks the other supervisors an estimation of their set size. Then it evaluates how to use the peers of its set to eventually balance the number of peers in each sets. Finally it sends to each peers of its set the identifier of their new set. Then, they insert themselves in the other sets. After this operation is finished, peers updates the links they had to other sets as some are no more relevant.

Split. To be efficient, this operation is based on the error recovery mechanism of the underlying DHT system. In Peer to Peer systems like Chord, indexed data are replicated to prevent missing them when a client depart unexpectedly from the system. For each peer, objects are replicated on its nearest neighbor. When a peer leaves, its neighbor is naturally considered as the new owner of the key previously owned by the leaving peer. The goal of the implementation of Split is to use these redundant information to prevent most communications.

Each supervisor is assigned a number of peers to provide for the new set. Thus the new set will be composed of some peers of all sets. It chooses them in order to well spread them amongst its peers. The chosen peer then join the new set, keeping their old identifier in order to keep with them their knowledge. If there are gaps in this knowledge, they ask other sets using classical range queries.

4   Performance Evaluation

4.1   Methodology of Evaluation

Multi-set is evaluated using a dedicated event-driven simulator implemented in Ocaml. Each peers created the same number of requests by using the *generator of requests*. Requests stand for queries and updates. Queries are relative to ranges open on the right (like in *at least 32 free processors*) and with the left bound uniformly distributed over the keys space (see section 3.3). The underlying Peer to Peer architecture is Chord-like [11].

To evaluate such a system, two points of view are necessary. The user one, and the system one. Users are willing to obtain the fastest possible answer. The system tries not to consume too much resources and to prevent specific part of it to be overloaded. As the simulator is to be used for large systems, it simulates the network at high level, and thus the performance measure (e.g., to evaluate query resolution) is the number of messages exchanged. To accommodate the two points of view, the metrics are *Mean number of messages for requests (Query and Update)* and *Workload balance*.

Mean number of messages for requests gives a good indication of latency for users. Moreover the the less the exchanged messages are, the less the amount of resources are needed.

Workload balance is an indicator to verify if unpleasant situations occur, as a single peer that answers all the requests. As this system aims to work efficiently without dedicated hardware, it is necessary to well balance workload amongst peers.

Those values are measured by counting the number of messages for each request. Multi-set is compared with the two other limit approaches, i.e. a single DHT and total replication. Data for one DHT and total replication are obtained by simulation too. Simulation results confirm the models of the three approaches.

Simulation and model are shown for 1000 nodes, experimentation for 120 nodes. Such large values are chosen to evaluate the scalability of the approach for future large Grids.

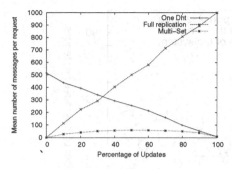
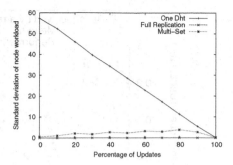

Fig. 5. Simulation of mean number of messages in a 1000 peers system to answer Queries and Update. X-axis shows the percentages of the requests that are Updates.

Fig. 6. Standard deviation of the peer's workload in a 1000 peers system. X-axis shows the percentages of the requests that are Updates one.

4.2   Dynamism of Keys

The following simulations where done with different scenarios, the limit case with only Queries requests to the other limit case with only Updates.

Figure 5 compares performances of the three methods for a network of 1000 peers as a function of the ratio Updates/Requests. Multi-set performance is always better than the others, particularly for non-extreme values of the ratio. The worst performance obtained for the Multi-set is when ratio is $1/2$. Yet, at this point it is more than 4 times more efficient than the system based on a single DHT, and 8 times more than the one based on total replication. This behavior confirms the model shown in Section 3.3.

Figure 6 compares standard deviation of the workload assigned to each peer for the three methods for uniformly distributed requests. Standard deviation of the total-replication is null as all the peers do always the same amount of work. Open queries for one DHT put a lot of weight on peers responsible for the end of the range. By using Multi-set, work is more distributed, even when there are mostly queries.

4.3   Dynamism of the Ratio

Our approach is efficient because it does not need to have an a priori estimation for the number of sets. This number evolves in function of the ratio Updates/Requests by using the basic operations Merge and Split.

Figure 7 shows the use of the Split operation in a system of 1000 peers. At the beginning, ratio is .8, then it changes to .5. At this point performance drops. After some data sent to the supervisor, one of these decides to run a Split to improve the overall performances.

It is worth noting that the performance, expressed as the mean number of messages to answer a request, gets worse and reaches a peak when the ratio changes. This occurs until the Split operations ends up by including an optimal number of sets. In this case three Splits are done to obtain the optimal number of sets.

As shown on the model (figure 4) the system performance is the worst one when the ratio is 0.5. Thus, the performance decreases during the ratio changes from 0.8 to 0.5.

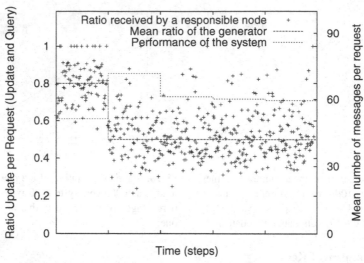

Fig. 7. Simulation of the set number evolution according to the ratio Updates/Requests (1000 peers). Left Y-axis is the ratio (dots and large dashes). Dots are the ratio values sent to supervisors. Large dashes is the mean value of these ratio. Right Y-axis (light dashes) is the performance (mean number of messages per request). Performance decrease when ratio changes, then the system adapts the set number to improve performance.

4.4 Experimental Validation

Testing our system on a real platform would validate the previous simulations and model. Using a real production Grid would limit the exploration of possible values for ratio and the nodes number. Moreover it would require a complete implementation of the Multi-set DHT, which would focus the performance evaluation on the underlying DHT rather than on the Multi-set itself. For these reasons, a simpler implementation of Multi-set is evaluated. It runs on PlanetLab which provides a distributed infrastructure that is comparable to the infrastructure linking local Resource Managers to real Grids. In this experimentation, the metric is the total time of execution. Compared to the previous simulations which only allow us to measure the number of exchanged messages, the results obtained by exploiting PlanetLab are more interesting. For example, they take into account also the real contents and size of messages.

For these experiments, 60 PlanetLab computers emulate the whole infrastructure. To be able to experiment on larger scale, several peers run on each physical computer of PlanetLab. During experimentations, each peers on a computer belongs to a different set. This is done to prevent local communications from occurring inside a single computer between peers. Such communications would be a bias as peers are supposed to be on different computers.

There are several available implementations of DHT[14,11]. Most of them do not implement range requests and only manage classical Hash Table. A good and efficient implementation of classical DHT without range queries, like Bamboo[14], is 20000 lines of Java and require heavy environments like a Java Virtual Machine (JVM) which becomes troublesome when running several peers on each computer.

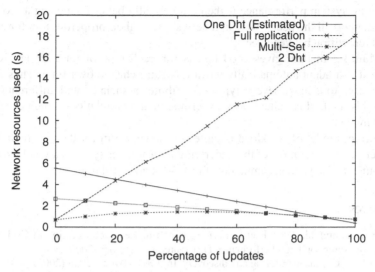

Fig. 8. Experimentation on PlanetLab using 60 computers to emulate 120 nodes. Multi-set is used with the number of sets ranging from 2 to 20 sets.

We implemented a light range enabled chord-like system in 1200 lines of python. Our implementation is aimed at providing basic range enabled DHT system with low requirements (no JVM by instance) and ease of modification to simplify obtaining traces of execution. This naive implementation does not yet manage the dynamism of nodes by instance.

Each peer can reply to range query requests, and can also generate requests, as in the previous simulation tests. Two metrics are used: *Mean number of communication per request* and *Total time of communication per request*.

During the 264 experiments, the first metric follows the model and simulation results. Total time of communication measures the global use of resources. Figure 8 shows that the experimental behavior roughly matches the simulations one. The main difference is that communications caused by range queries are more expensive than the one due to updates. In our experiment, range communication take 50% more time as they transport more information. This lead to a slight change of the optimal number of sets according to the ratio, but this can be included easily in the model by increasing the weight of queries. In comparison to the simulation and emulation results, full replication turns out to be less efficient, and this is due to the broad latencies distribution in PlanetLab.

5   Conclusion

Most of the Peer to Peer systems able to answer range queries directly try to solve the problem by optimizing the Query and the Update costs. We choose to address a more realistic case where the ratio between the queries and updates is important. Our approach can be used to improve the perfomance of a P2P system able to answer range queries. In particular, since our proposal requires to partition all the participating nodes in several sets, the same P2P network organization can be exploited within each set.

The resulting system performance is then dramatically better than using a global P2P system spanning all the peers. We can inherit some of their properties too, for example workload repartition between peers.

The Multi-set method gives good results for each type of ratio Update/Request. Moreover it can adapt automatically when this ratio change over time. Thus this can efficiently used to manage several types of attributes associated with different Grid resources. This method is validated by experiments and simulations which confirm the proposed model.

The current model of workload is quite simple (uniform for the first bound of the range query). However most of the underlying Peer to Peer systems are able to modify the assignment of keys to accommodate fair workload distribution.

References

1. Foster, I., Iamnitchi, A.: A Peer-to-Peer Approach to Resource Location in Grid Environments. In: Symp. on High Performance Distributed Computing (2002)
2. Clifford, B.: Globus monitoring and discovery. In: GlobusWorld 2005 (2005)
3. Costa, G.D., Orlando, S., Dikaiakos, M.D.: Multi-set DHT for interval queries on dynamic data. Coregrid Technical report TR-0084 (2007)
4. Oppenheimer, D.P.D., Albrecht, J., Vahdat, A.: Scalable wide-area resource discovery. Technical Report UCB/CSD-04-1334, EECS Department, University of California, Berkeley (2004)
5. Ganesan, P., Bawa, M., Garcia-Molina, H.: Online balancing of range-partitioned data with applications to peer-to-peer systems. Technical report, Stanford U (2004)
6. Gribble, S.D., Halevy, A.Y., Ives, Z.G., Rodrig, M., Suciu, D.: What can database do for peer-to-peer? In: Fourth International Workshop on the Web and Databases (WebDB 2001), pp. 31–336 (2001)
7. Jagadish, H.V., Ooi, B.C., Vu, Q.H.: Baton: a balanced tree structure for peer-to-peer networks. In: VLDB 2005: Proceedings of the 31st international conference on Very large data bases, pp. 661–672. VLDB Endowment (2005)
8. Ntarmos, N., Pitoura, T., Triantafillou, P.: Range query optimization leveraging peer heterogeneity. In: Moro, G., Bergamaschi, S., Joseph, S., Morin, J.-H., Ouksel, A.M. (eds.) DBISP2P 2005 and DBISP2P 2006. LNCS, vol. 4125. Springer, Heidelberg (2007)
9. Oram, A.: Peer-to-Peer: Harnessing the Power of Disruptive Technologies. O'Reilly, Sebastopol (2001)
10. Sahin, O.D., Antony, S., Agrawal, D., El Abbadi, A.: Probe: Multi-dimensional range queries in p2p networks. In: Ngu, A.H.H., Kitsuregawa, M., Neuhold, E.J., Chung, J.-Y., Sheng, Q.Z. (eds.) WISE 2005. LNCS, vol. 3806, pp. 332–346. Springer, Heidelberg (2005)
11. Stoica, I., Morris, R., Karger, D., Kaashoek, F., Balakrishnan, H.: Chord: A scalable peer-to-peer lookup service for internet applications. Technical Report TR-819, MIT (March 2001)
12. Trunfio, P., Talia, D., Fragopoulou, P., Papadakis, C., Mordacchini, M., Pennanen, M., Popov, K., Vlassov, V., Haridi, S.: Peer-to-peer models for resource discovery on grids. In: Proc. of the 2nd CoreGRID Workshop on Grid and Peer to Peer Systems Architecture (2006)
13. Karger, D.R., Ruhl, M.: Simple Efficient Load Balancing Algorithms for Peer-to-Peer Systems. In: SPAA 2004: Proceedings of the sixteenth annual ACM Symposium on Parallelism in Algorithms and Architectures (2004)
14. Rhea, S., Godfrey, B., Karp, B., Kubiatowicz, J., Ratnasamy, S., Shenker, S., Stoica, I., Yu, H.: OpenDHT: A Public DHT Service and Its Uses. In: Proceedings of ACM SIGCOMM 2005 (August 2005)

Experimenting the Query Performance of a Grid-Based Sensor Network Data Warehouse

Alfredo Cuzzocrea[1], Abhas Kumar[2,*], and Vincenzo Russo[1]

[1] ICAR Institute and DEIS Department,
University of Calabria, Italy
{cuzzocrea,russo}@si.deis.unical.it
[2] Department of Computer Science and Engineering,
Indian Institute of Technology, Kanpur, India
abhas@cse.iitk.ac.in

Abstract. This paper presents our experience in experimenting the query performance of a Grid-based sensor network data warehouse, which encompasses several metaphors of data compression/approximation and high performance and high reliability computing that are typical of Grid architectures. Our experimentation focuses on two main classes of aggregate range queries over sensor readings, namely (*i*) the window queries, which apply a SQL aggregation operator over a fixed window over the reading stream produced by the sensor network, and (*ii*) the continuous queries, which instead consider a "moving" window, and produce as output a stream of answers. Both classes of queries are extremely useful to extract summarized knowledge to be exploited by OLAP-like analysis tools over sensor network data. The experimental results, conducted on several synthetic data sets, clearly confirm the benefits deriving from embedding the data compression/approximation paradigm into Grid-based sensor network data warehouses.

1 Introduction

Grid Data Warehouses (GDWH) [27,30,7,31,29,24,21] combine data representation and management functionalities of consolidated *Data Warehousing* (DW) methodologies [8], such as data integration, data consolidation, data loading and refreshing, storage primitives, metadata management and indexing routines, with high performance and high reliability of *Grid Computing* [16,15].

Sensor network data management and analysis is a typical context where GDWH technology can effectively provide facilities during all the phases, ranging from sensor reading collection, storage and processing to OLAP [18] query evaluation over materialized sensor readings [11,12,24]. Particularly, the opportunity of storing, handling and querying materialized sensor readings in a multi-dimensional fashion puts the basis for a novel class of *Intelligent Information Systems over Grids*, the so-called

---

* Work done during a summer internship at the Institute of High Performance Computing and Networking of the Italian National Research Council.

A. Hameurlain (Ed.): Globe 2008, LNCS 5187, pp. 105–119, 2008.

Grid OLAP [22,23,14,5]. This vision is opposite to other classical approaches that instead pursue the goal of efficiently processing and querying sensor readings *in an online manner* [17,13,26,10].

Despite high performance and high reliability of Grid architectures, handling sensor network data in GDWH still represents a research challenge due to high dimensionality and massive size of readings produced by large sensor networks. A possible solution to the deriving limitations is represented by the *data compression and approximation paradigm*, which has already demonstrated its effectiveness and efficiency in the context of *approximate query answering over large databases and data cubes* [3]. Inspired by these motivations, in [11,12] *SensorGrid*, a Grid-based sensor network data warehouse that founds on the data compression/approximation paradigm, is presented, along with maintenance and query algorithms. Moreover, to efficiency purposes *SensorGrid* makes use of *approximate aggregate query answering techniques over data streams* (such as sensor readings) introduced in [10] in order to deal with the unbounded nature of streaming data.

In this paper, we provide a comprehensive experimental evaluation of the *Sensor-Grid* query performance for two important classes of OLAP-like queries over sensor readings, namely the *window queries* [10] and *continuous queries* [4]. Window queries apply a SQL aggregation operator over a fixed window over the materialized sensor readings (i.e., in an OLAP-like manner). Continuous queries instead consider a "moving" window, and produce as output a *stream of answers*. Both classes of queries are extremely useful to extract *summarized knowledge* to be further exploited by OLAP-like analysis tools over sensor network data. Also, the experimental assessment we propose is conducted on several synthetic data sets, and takes into account several perspectives of performance analysis. The experimental results clearly confirm the benefits deriving from embedding the data compression/approximation paradigm into Grid-based sensor network data warehouses.

The remaining part of this paper is organized as follows. In Sect. 2, we review related work. Sect. 3 provides an overview of *SensorGrid*. Sect. 4 is devoted to the approximate aggregate query answering techniques proposed in [10]. In Sect. 5, we provide the main contribution of this paper, i.e. a comprehensive experimental evaluation of *SensorGrid* query performance for both window and continuous queries, along with a critical analysis of retrieved results. Finally, in Sect. 6 we complete our contribution with conclusions of our research and guidelines for future efforts in this research field.

2   Related Work

Although DW research issues have been widely investigated in the context of conventional architectures (e.g., client-server), surprisingly there is not much work in literature that focuses on how to efficiently support GDWH. Contrary to this, Grid architecture features are indeed appealing for the development and management of large and high-dimensional Data Warehouses. Basically, in order to implement a (distributed) Data Warehouse on the Grid, one must start from *OGSA-DAI* [2] primitives realizing common DW operations such as extraction, cleaning, integration, load and refresh, indexing etc. In this respect, distributed query processing [28] plays a crucial role for what regards the proper query layer but also the data integration layer without active behaviors such as data placement and replication. In this direction, [25] carefully studies the integration between databases and Grids, and proposes guidelines for the achievement of effective and efficient Grid-enabled databases, which can be reasonably considered as a first step towards GDWH.

[21] proposes the guidelines of an architecture for devising a *Distributed Hetero-geneous Relational Data Warehouse* (DHRD) over the Grid, which is indeed based on *Web services* and the *virtualization* of commercial DBMS platforms such as *SQL Server* and *Oracle 9i*. On top of this GDWH architecture, [21] develops a scientific computing software environment for supporting high energy and nuclear physics experimentations. [30] proposes a *chunk-based* approach for efficiently implementing GDWH, and devises models and algorithms for distributing and querying the GDWH effectively. [7] again considers fragments and replicated fragments in order to realize the GDWH. The novelty of [7] relies in a prediction model that is used in conjunction with QoS policies in order to enable the establishment of *Service Level Agreements* (SLA). [31] proposes to improve common operations that can be performed in a GDWH by means of a global data localization method aided by a specialized catalog service. This service makes use of *local indexes* over materialized data in order to support efficient *cost-based query execution plans*. [24] proposes an interesting GDWH architecture for *continuous data stream processing*. The main idea of this approach consists in providing the design guidelines of the so-called *Grid-based Zero-Latency Data Stream Warehouse* (GZLDSWH), which overcomes resource limitations of conventional architectures in answering queries over (potentially-unbounded) data streams without introducing approximation.

Grid OLAP architectures have recently received considerable attention from the Database and Data Warehousing research communities. This novel perspective of GDWH research poses unrecognized challenges ranging from distribution and frag-mentation to integration and query models on multidimensional data over the Grid. Among most recent proposals, we recall: (*i*) [22,23], which provide a model for the so-called *OLAP-enabled Grid* that makes use of collaborative caching to reduce data transmission, aggregation and recombination costs dictated by handling data cubes distributed across the Grid; (*ii*) *GridMiner* [14,5], which is a knowledge discovery infrastructure for Grid databases that makes an extensive use of the OLAP technology to integrate, process and discovery knowledge kept in these databases.

Among commercial platforms, [27] develops a DW solution on Grids on top of Grid-enabled databases of static data, without considering important capabilities of Data Grids such as dynamic placement and replication (e.g., [1]).

Finally, for what regards application scenarios, [29] employs GDWH to fold and unfold molecular dynamics of proteins. The latter can be reasonably considered as a successful case demonstrating the significant impact of GDWH on real-life complex data-intensive systems and applications.

3 *SensorGrid*: A Grid-Based Sensor Network Data Warehouse

SensorGrid [11,12] is a Grid framework for managing sensor network data and sup-porting approximate aggregate query answering on summarized readings produced by

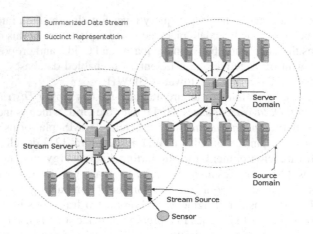

Fig. 1. *SensorGrid* logical overview

features [16,15], such as high performance, large-scale resource sharing, data reliability etc. Therefore, *SensorGrid* realizes a commonly-intended GDWH, but targeted to sensor network data.

SensorGrid consists of the following entities (see Fig. 1): (*i*) *Sensor*: is the basic data source; (*ii*) *Stream Source*: is the Grid node collecting readings produced by sensors; (*iii*) *Source Domain*: is a domain of *Stream Sources*; (*iv*) *Stream Server*: is the Grid node handling the summarized information stored in a certain *Source Domain*; (*v*) *Server Domain*: is a domain of *Stream Servers* that establish a *subscriber/executor snapshot protocol*, called *Grid Snapshot Protocol* (*GSP*). According to the architecture sketched above, *SensorGrid* is based on the definition of several domains at different levels of abstraction, and each of these domains is responsible for a particular task. The final goal of such an approach is to obtain a *multi-level* Grid framework able to efficiently manage and analyze readings produced by high dimensional and high performance sensor networks.

In order to efficiently support approximate aggregate query answering on sensor readings, we adopt a *two-dimensional aggregation scheme* for representing summarized readings, first proposed in [10]. Under this scheme, the first dimension, called *sensor dimension*, represents the sensor domain, and the other one, called *temporal dimension*, represents the time. Each cell of the so-obtained two-dimensional array stores the *sum* of all the readings produced by the corresponding range of sensors during the corresponding time interval. Specifically, due to the aggregation function considered, it is clear that this approach addresses the problem of efficiently evaluating *range-SUM aggregate queries* [20], which apply the SQL aggregation operator *SUM* on a set of selected data. However, this is not an important limitation of our representation model, as supporting *SUM*-based aggregations allows us to also manage *AVG*- and *COUNT*-based aggregations as well. It should be noted that these three aggregation operators altogether are very useful to a large number of large-scale scientific applications, such as those focused on data management activities in the aerospace, environmental, networked and telecommunication contexts. Indeed, all these application contexts are usually characterized by a sensor network infrastructure devoted to collect and handle streaming and transactional readings, for which extracting summarized knowledge for decision making purposes plays a critical role. An overview of the approximate aggregate query answering technique [10] is provided in Sect. 4.

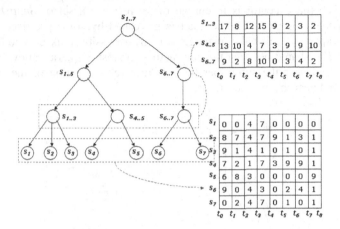

Fig. 2. *AH* and *MAS*

SensorGrid further extends the previous approach [10] via *improving the semantics of the sensor dimension*. In fact, while the temporal dimension can be aggregated by means of several strategies (e.g., *Minute* → *Hour* → *Day* or *Week* → *Month* → *Year*), as time is naturally ordered, the sensor dimension is not naturally ordered and then an *enumeration* (e.g., based on the absolute sensor identifier) must be introduced. This is the main assumption of the proposal [10]. Nevertheless, for many real-life sensor network applications, *defining an aggregation hierarchy on the sensor set is mandatory*. For instance, a *Geographic Information System (GIS)* for weather forecasting significantly depends on the definition of such a hierarchy on the sensor domain. To adequately fulfill this lack, in *SensorGrid* the evolution of the original aggregation scheme [10] is achieved via *superimposing an Aggregation Hierarchy (AH) on the sensor domain*. *AH* is finally implemented as a *general tree* where leaf nodes represent sensors, and internal nodes represent aggregations of sensors, *following a given semantics*. Hence, *AH* must be defined in dependence on the particular application scenario considered, and stored in the target *Stream Server* handling that domain of sensors. *AH* allows us to obtain a *Multi-Level Aggregation Scheme (MAS)* over the whole two-dimensional sensor-time domain of aggregate readings (see Fig. 2), which is a significant evolution of the previous (single-level) aggregation scheme [10]. In particular, each level ℓ of the *AH* involves in a specific aggregation partition of the summarized readings where sensors are aggregated according to ℓ, and the time range is kept unaltered (see Fig. 2). This amenity allows us to take advantages from an OLAP-like multi-resolution manner of representing and querying the examined sensor readings.

Another important component of *SensorGrid* is represented by the *GSP* (see Fig. 3). On the basis of this Grid-oriented data exchange protocol, a *Stream Server* S_i maintains a *succinct version* of summarized readings stored in another *Stream Server* S_j (see Fig. 1), and exploits it at query time. Specifically, in the *GSP* two roles are introduced, namely the *Snapshot Executor* and the *Snapshot Subscriber*. These roles are played by *Stream Servers* that establish the so-called *Snapshot Contract*, on the basis of which the executor is in charge of performing a set of *Snapshot Queries* required by the subscriber. The contract is governed by some pre-fixed rules (e.g., execution frequency, null value management, transmission bulk etc) codified into a *Snapshot Policy* shared between the contractors. Snapshot queries allow us to obtain (or refresh, too) near the subscriber the succinct representation of the summarized readings stored near the executor (see Fig. 3).

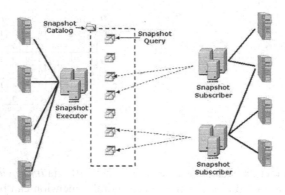

Fig. 3. *GSP*

GSP is meant to support both data and replica management facilities (e.g., load balancing, fault tolerance etc), but mostly a distributed query evaluation paradigm based on the *approximation concept*. Under this vision, during the evaluation of an OLAP query Q posed to a server S_i and involving the domain of summarized readings handled by another server S_j, S_i can alternatively (1) re-direct Q towards the responsible server S_j, or (2) answer Q by using its local succinct representation of summarized readings stored in S_j, thus providing a less-detailed answer, or (3) decompose Q in a subset of queries $\{q_0, q_1, ..., q_{N-1}\}$ to be executed in another set of Grid nodes based on their own succinct representations of summarized readings stored in S_j. The above-described query scenario leads to the definition of the so-called *Grid-aware Distributed Query Engine (GaDQE)*. The main functionality carried out by *GaDQE* consists in dynamically determining cost-based optimal distributed query execution plans on top of (*i*) "traditional" parameters such arrival rate, transmission bandwidth, Grid nodes computational power, load balancing issues etc, and (*ii*) the approximation paradigm, i.e. the amenity of querying a certain Grid node or a set of Grid nodes instead of the original one on the basis of the required approximation degree and summarized reading replicas.

4 Approximate Aggregate Query Answering on Summarized Sensor Readings

In order to provide fast approximate answers to aggregate queries on sensor readings, *SensorGrid* embeds the framework proposed in [10]. This framework, oriented to streaming data, is general enough to include sensor readings as a specialized instance of more general data streams. Briefly, the proposal [10] is based on a *quad-tree based hierarchical summarization* of data streams over *fixed time windows*, called *Quad-Tree Windows* (*QTW*), implemented by means of conventional quad-trees and embedded into a flexible *B*-tree indexing data structure. At the lowest level of aggregation, a *QTW* represents summarized readings into two-dimensional sensor-time arrays (see Sect. 3). The whole collection of *QTW* plus the *B*-tree index form the so-called *Multi-Resolution Data Stream Summary* (*MRDS*). In *SensorGrid*, *Stream Servers* store *MRDS* data structures as summarized representations of readings produced by sensors belonging to *their own Source Domains* (see Fig. 1). Also, *Stream Servers* store *MRDS* data structures as succinct representations of readings produced by sensor belonging to *other Source Domains* (see Fig. 1). Each (native) *MRDS* is progressively compressed meaning that it is updated continuously, as new sensor readings arrive, and, when the available storage space is not enough to host new data into "newest" *QTW*, some space is released via compressing the "oldest" *QTW*. By adopting this approach, the recent knowledge on the *MRDS* is represented with more detail than the old one. Note that the recent knowledge is usually more relevant to extract for the context of sensor network applications. Fig. 4 shows a sketch of the *MRDS* data structure.

Using such a representation, an estimate of the answer to a (general) range-SUM query $Q = \langle [S_s:S_e], [t_s:t_e] \rangle$ over summarized data streams, such that S_s and S_e are the starting and ending stream sources, respectively, and t_s and t_e are the starting and ending timestamps, respectively, can be obtained by summing two contributions. The first one is given by the sum of those ranges completely contained by the query range. The second one is given by the sum of those ranges that are partially contained by the query range. Note that the first of these contributions does not introduce any approximation, whereas the second one is approximate, as the use of the time granularity Δt_j makes impossible to discriminate the distribution of data streams within the

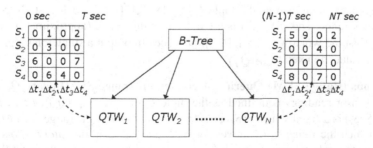

Fig. 4. *MRDS* overview

same interval Δt_j. Specifically, the latter contribution can be evaluated by means of well-known *linear interpolation techniques* [6], assuming that data distributions inside each range are uniform (see Fig. 5: the depicted gray box represents the range-SUM query $Q = \langle [S_1 : S_3], [5:15] \rangle$).

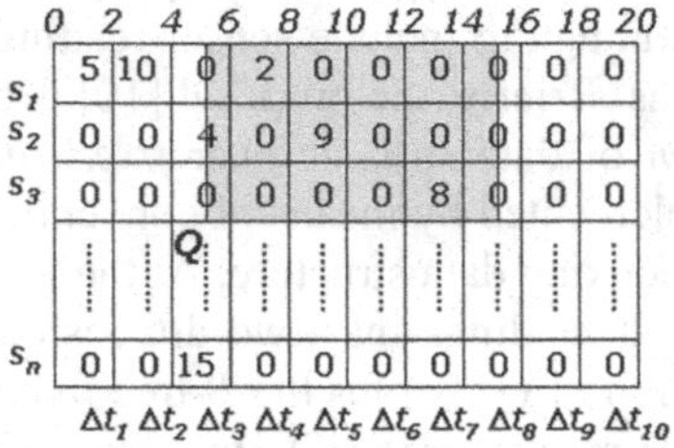

Fig. 5. Two-dimensional representation and querying of summarized readings

5 Experimental Evaluation

Preliminaries. In this Section, we present and discuss our experimental evaluation of the *SensorGrid* query performance for both window (range-SUM) queries and continuous (range-SUM) queries on synthetic data sets. First, note that, since our emphasis is on testing the *accuracy of approximation* due to the compression paradigm on materialized sensor readings (i.e., in an OLAP-like manner), in our experimentation we introduce an *error metrics* that considers the relative difference between the exact answer (i.e., the answer evaluated on the uncompressed sensor readings) and the approximate answer (i.e., the answer evaluated on the compressed sensor readings). Therefore, this imposes us to *run experiments on the compressed portions of the MRDS, and neglect the uncompressed MRDS portions accordingly.* As regards the experimental environment, we implemented a Java-based framework where sensor sources are modeled by Java threads, and located on different Grid nodes of the experimental architecture, which is composed by five *Stream Servers*, each one running *Gnu/Linux Fedora Core 6 OS* with *Globus Toolkit 3*, and equipped with *Intel Pentium IV* at 2 GHz processors and 1 GB RAM.

Window (Range-SUM) Queries. A window (range-SUM) query Q_W on summarized sensor readings is defined as the tuple $Q_W = \langle [S_s : S_e], [t_s : t_e] \rangle$, such that (i) $[S_s : S_e]$ is a fixed sensor range, and (ii) $[t_s : t_e]$ is a fixed time range. The (approximate) evaluation of Q_W against the window $\langle [S_s : S_e], [t_s : t_e] \rangle$ produces in output a singleton (approximate) aggregate value, denoted by $\tilde{A}(Q_W)$.

Continuous (Range-SUM) Queries. A continuous (range-SUM) query Q_C on summarized sensor readings is defined as the tuple $Q_C = \langle \langle [S_s : S_e], [t_s : t_e] \rangle, \Delta t_{step}, f_Q \rangle$, such that (i) $[S_s : S_e]$ is a fixed sensor range, (ii) $[t_s : t_e]$ is a *moving* time range, (iii) Δt_{step} is the step by which the range $[t_s : t_e]$ moves forward, and (v) f_Q is the *query frequency* that establishes the time period by which Q_C is evaluated as a window query on the *actual* window $\langle [S_s : S_e], [t_s + \Delta t_{step} \times k : t_e + \Delta t_{step} \times k] \rangle$, at the iteration k. This produces in output a stream of answers.

Data Sets. In order to carefully test the query performance of *SensorGrid* under the stress of a "ranging" input, we considered two kinds of data sets. This allows us to obtain a more reliable experimental evaluation. Data sets considered are the following ones: synthetic and real-life data sets. Experimental results are similar for both classes of data sets. Therefore, for space reasons, in this paper we present the results obtained from synthetic data sets. To generate synthetic data sets, we used customizable data distributions characterizing the nature of (synthetic) sensor readings. In particular, we introduced three distributions: (*i*) *Uniform*, which models sensor readings whose values are uniformly distributed over a given interval; (*ii*) *Gauss*, which models sensor readings whose values are distributed according to a Gaussian distribution; (*iii*) *Zipf*, which models sensor readings whose values are distributed according to a Zipfian distribution, with parameter *z* uniformly distributed over a given interval. It should be noted that these distributions are together able to capture the most popular cases of sensor reading distributions that one can finds in real-life sensor networks. The benefits deriving from using synthetic data sets mainly rely in the possibility of completely controlling the nature of such data sets, thus better studying how the query performance of the system varies with respect to the variation of characteristics of the input data set.

Error Metrics. We introduce a different error metrics in dependence on the kind of queries considered. For window queries, we consider synthetically-generated populations of range queries over the compressed portion of the *MRDS*. This portion, which in our model is delimited by the value T_{max} on the temporal dimension, can be easily determined during the run of the experimental framework via monitoring when the compression process is activated. Let $\langle[S_0{:}S_{N-1}], [t_0{:}T_{max}]\rangle$ denote the compressed portion of the *MRDS*, and ΔS and ΔT two input parameters that represent a range on the sensor dimension and a range on the temporal dimension, respectively. We obtained the population of window queries QP_W as those queries contained by the range $\langle[S_0{:}S_{N-1}], [t_0{:}T_{max}]\rangle$, and having (*i*) *selectivity* equal to $\Delta S \times \Delta T$ and (*ii*) left-up corners corresponding with items of the range $\langle[S_0{:}S_{N-1}], [t_0{:}T_{max}]\rangle$. To establish how much window queries generate, and hence the cardinality of QP_W, denoted by $|QP_W|$, we introduce the *sampling factor s* that determines a sample of the "maximal" query population $QP_{W,MAX}$ (for which $s = 100$ %). $QP_{W,MAX}$ is that population that can be defined on the range $\langle[S_0{:}S_{N-1}], [t_0{:}T_{max}]\rangle$ via considering queries having as left-up corners corresponding to *all* the items of the range $\langle[S_0{:}S_{N-1}], [t_0{:}T_{max}]\rangle$. Upon this model, we introduce the error metrics given by the *Average Relative Error* ε_{QP_W},

defined as follows: $\varepsilon_{QP_W} = \dfrac{1}{|QP_W|} \cdot \sum_{k=0}^{|QP_W|-1} \varepsilon(Q_{W,k})$, such that $\varepsilon(Q_{W,k})$ is the relative

error due to the approximate evaluation of the window query $Q_{W,k}$. In turn, $\varepsilon(Q_{W,k})$ is

defined as follows: $\varepsilon(Q_{W,k}) = \dfrac{|A(Q_{W,k}) - \tilde{A}(Q_{W,k})|}{A(Q_{W,k})}$, where $A(Q_{W,k})$ is the exact answer

to $Q_{W,k}$, and $\tilde{A}(Q_{W,k})$ is the approximate answer to $Q_{W,k}$.

For continuous queries, we instead fix both the (query) range on the sensor dimension, ΔS, and the (query) range on the temporal dimension, ΔT, and moves forward the $\Delta S \times \Delta T$ window query by steps equal to Δt_{step}, being the latter one an input parameter. The (approximate) answer is evaluated with frequency f_Q. Due to the particular nature of continuous queries, in this case we do not adopt an averaged value as metrics (like in window queries), but rather we observe how "distant" is the variation of the approximate answer from the one of the exact one, and the corresponding relative error. Also, we consider two distinct queries simultaneously. The first one is a "small" query, i.e. a query having low selectivity, and the second one is a "large" query, i.e. a query having high selectivity. It is well-recognized that query selectivity heavily impacts on the performance of any query engine.

Other Experimental Parameters. Beyond the parameters introduced above (i.e., T_{max} and s), the following ones characterize our experimental framework: (i) N, which is the number of sensor sources; (ii) Δt, which is the granularity of the system (denoted as dt in the following figures); (iii) p, which is the depth of the B-tree embedded into the *MRDS*. Moreover, synthetic data sets are termed by the string $F_1F_2F_3$ (denoted as *dist* in the following figures), such that (i) F_1 is the distribution associated to the *topology* of the sensor network, (ii) F_2 is the distribution associated to the sensor reading values, and (iii) F_3 is the distribution associated to the simulation time of the experimental framework. Every distribution F_i, with i in $\{1, 2, 3\}$, can assume the following values: (i) U, which means that the Uniform distribution is employed; (ii) G, which means that the Gaussian distribution is employed; (iii) Z, which means that the Zipfian distribution is employed. In our experimental assessment, we notice that the best performance is achieved with $F_1 = U$ and $F_3 = U$, so that in this paper we show such kind of experiments. However, our experimental framework is general enough to cope with any distribution modeling all the concepts from sensors to readings and simulation time.

For what instead regards parameters related to the analysis of experimental results (i.e., how results are visualized into plots), we again adopt different strategies in dependence on the kind of queries (window or continuous). For window queries, we observe the variation of the percentage value of ε_{QP_W} with respect to the selectivity of queries belonging to the population QP_W, given by the pair $\{\Delta S, \Delta T\}$, and with respect to the compression ratio r, which models the percentage occupancy of the compressed *MRDS* with respect to the uncompressed *MRDS*. For continuous queries, we observe the "relative" variations of exact and approximate answers to "small" and "large" queries, and the variation of the percentage value of the corresponding $\varepsilon(Q_W)$, all with respect to time.

Experimental Results. Fig. 6 shows the experimental results when considering window queries as input. Fig. 7 instead shows the case for continuous queries. In particular, Fig. 6 (a) shows the variation of the percentage value of ε_{QP_W} with respect to the selectivity of (window) queries in QP_W on an Uniform (synthetic) data set (i.e., $F_2 = U$), with the following configuration of the experimental parameters: $\{N = 64, T_{max} = 51,200, \Delta t = 25, p = 2, s = 100\ \%\}$ (recall that $F_1 = U$ and $F_3 = U$). Fig. 6 (b) shows the same experimentation when ranging the compression ratio r. Fig. 6 (c) and Fig. 6 (d) show the above-illustrated metrics for a Gaussian (synthetic) data set (i.e., $F_2 = G$), whereas Fig. 6 (e) and Fig. 6 (f) for a Zipfian (synthetic) data set (i.e., $F_2 = Z$). Fig. 7 (a) focuses on the variation of the "distance" between exact and approximate answers to two "small" and "large" (continuous) queries on an Uniform (synthetic) data set (i.e., $F_2 = U$). Fig. 7 (b) plots the percentage variation of $\varepsilon(Q_C)$ due to exact and approximate answers shown in Fig. 7 (a). Finally, Fig. 7 (c) and Fig. 7 (d), and Fig. 7 (e) and Fig. 7 (f) show the same experimentation on a Gaussian (synthetic) data set (i.e., $F_2 = G$), and a Zipfian (synthetic) data set (i.e., $F_2 = Z$), respectively. It should be noted that for continuous queries, a different configuration of the experimental parameters has been considered, due to need for (i) adequately testing with continuous queries (this involved $p = 3$), and (ii) capturing the starting time of the related *MRDS* compression process (this involved $T_{max} = 75,225$ for the Uniform data set, and $T_{max} = 75,133$ for Gaussian and Zipfian data sets).

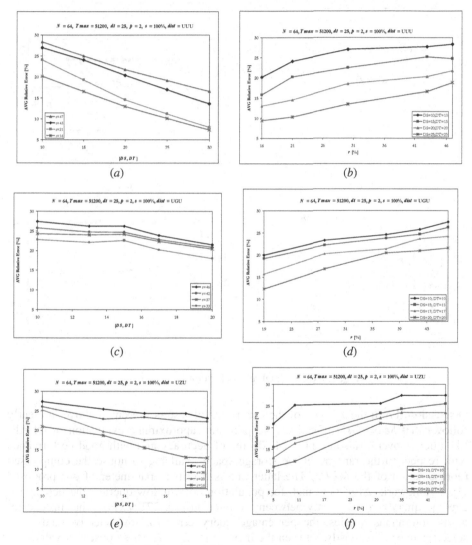

Fig. 6. Experimental results for window queries

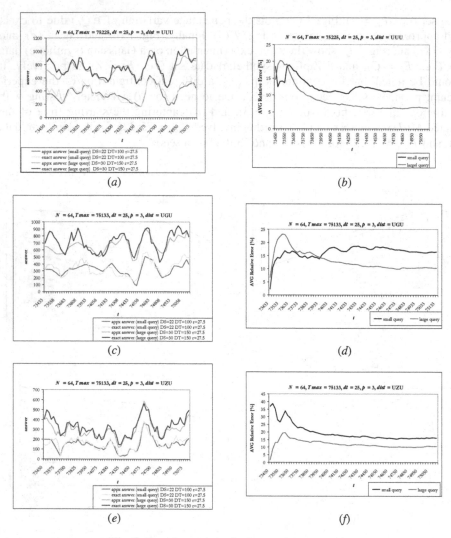

Fig. 7. Experimental results for continuous queries

Discussion. From the analysis of the experimental results presented above, it clearly follows that *SensorGrid* effectively supports the approximate evaluation of OLAP-like queries over Grids at a provable degree of accuracy and with good performance with respect to the ranging of the storage space available to house the compressed representation of the *MRDS*. The latter one is a critical parameter of our proposed Grid framework. Also, note that, for populations of window queries, the percentage average query error is mostly between the interval [10, 27] %. For what instead regards continuous queries, the percentage query error for low-selective and high-selective queries is mostly between the interval [5, 20] %. These observed values are well-recognized as *best performance* for *any* approximate query engine over OLAP data (e.g., [9]).

Indeed, the latter capability is of farthest interest because of several knowledge discovery tasks, such as *OnLine Analytical Mining* (OLAM) and *Complex Data Mining Activities* (CDMA), are typically resource-intensive and strictly demand for highly-efficient baseline primitives and routines. This evidence gets worse when OLAM and CDMA are applied in the probing context of sensor network data processing over Grids within the broader scope of GDWH. In this respect, it should be noted that evaluating both window and continuous queries over such kind of data streams is the most costing operation for the above-mentioned tasks, so that our data compression/approximation approach, whose effectiveness has been demonstrated by the previous experimental results, finally results to be an "enabling" technology for GDWH.

6 Conclusions and Future Work

This paper has reported our experience with the experimental assessment of the query performance of *SensorGrid*, a Grid-based sensor network data warehouse that founds on the data compression/approximation paradigm. The experimental evaluation has been conducted on several synthetic data sets, and with regard to both window and continuous OLAP-like queries, which are very useful to extract summarized knowledge from large amounts of materialized readings stored in Grid nodes. This knowledge is in turn extremely helpful to decision support purposes in the context of data-intensive sensor network applications. Indeed, knowledge kept in these applications cannot be successfully fruited neither exploited by means of conventional DBMS-inspired analysis tools. Future work is mainly oriented towards two research efforts: (*i*) making *SensorGrid* capable of dealing with *multidimensional sensor readings*, which arise in several novel application contexts (e.g., [19]); (*ii*) making *SensorGrid* capable of supporting innovative classes of meaningful queries based on *complex predicates* (e.g., [17,13]) over sensor readings.

References

1. Allcock, W.E., Bester, J., Bresnahan, J., Chervenak, A.L., Foster, I.T., Kesselman, C., Meder, S., Nefedova, V., Quesnel, D., Tuecke, S.: Data Management and Transfer in High-Performance Computational Grid Environments. Parallel Computing 28(5), 749–77 (2002)
2. Antonioletti, M., Atkinson, M., Baxter, R., Borley, A., Chue Hong, N., Collins, B., Hardman, N., Hume, A., Knox, A., Jackson, M., Krause, A., Laws, S., Magowan, J., Paton, N.W., Pearson, D., Sugden, T., Watson, P., Westhead, M.: The Design and Implementation of Grid Database Services in OGSA-DAI. Concurrency and Computation: Practice and Experience 17(2-4), 357–376 (2005)
3. Barbara, D., DuMouchel, W., Faloutsos, C., Haas, P.J., Hellerstein, J.M., Ioannidis, Y.E., Jagadish, H.V., Johnson, T., Ng, R.T., Poosala, V., Ross, K.A., Sevcik, K.C.: The New Jersey Data Reduction Report. IEEE Data Engineering Bulletin 20(4), 3–45 (1997)
4. Babu, S., Widom, J.: Continuous Queries over Data Streams. ACM SIGMOD Record 30(3), 109–120 (2001)

5. Brezany, P., Janciak, I., Tjoa, A.M.: GridMiner: A Fundamental Infrastructure for Building Intelligent Grid Systems. IEEE/ACM WI, 150–156 (2005)
6. Buccafurri, F., Furfaro, F., Saccà, D., Sirangelo, C.: A Quad-Tree based Multiresolution Approach for Two-Dimensional Summary Data. IEEE SSDBM, 127–140 (2003)
7. de Carvalho Costa, R.L., Furtado, P.: An SLA-Enabled Grid Data Warehouse. IEEE IDEAS, 285–289 (2007)
8. Chaudhuri, S., Dayal, U.: An Overview of Data Warehousing and OLAP Technology. ACM SIGMOD Record 26(1), 65–74 (1997)
9. Cuzzocrea, A.: Overcoming Limitations of Approximate Query Answering in OLAP. IEEE IDEAS, 200–209 (2005)
10. Cuzzocrea, A., Furfaro, F., Masciari, E., Saccà, D., Sirangelo, C.: Approximate Query Answering on Sensor Network Data Streams. In: Stefanidis, A., Nittel, S. (eds.) GeoSensor Networks, pp. 53–72. CRC Press, Boca Raton (2004)
11. Cuzzocrea, A., Furfaro, F., Mazzeo, G.M., Saccà, D.: A Grid Framework for Approximate Aggregate Query Answering on Summarized Sensor Network Readings. GADA, 144–153 (2004)
12. Cuzzocrea, A., Furfaro, F., Greco, S., Mazzeo, G.M., Masciari, E., Saccà, D.: A Distributed System for Answering Range Queries on Sensor Network Data. IEEE PerSeNS, 369–373 (2005)
13. Dobra, A., Gehrke, J., Garofalakis, M., Rastogi, R.: Processing Complex Aggregate Queries over Data Streams. ACM SIGMOD, 61–72 (2002)
14. Fiser, B., Onan, U., Elsayed, I., Brezany, P., Tjoa, A.M.: On-Line Analytical Processing on Large Databases Managed by Computational Grids. In: IEEE DEXA Workshops, pp. 556–560 (2004)
15. Foster, I., Kesselman, C., Nick, J.M., Tuecke, S.: Grid Services for Distributed System Integration. IEEE Computer 35(6), 37–46 (2002)
16. Foster, I., Kesselman, C., Tuecke, S.: The Anatomy of the Grid: Enabling Scalable Virtual Organizations. International Journal of High Performance Computing Applications 15(3), 200–222 (2001)
17. Gehrke, J., Korn, F., Srivastava, D.: On Computing Correlated Aggregates over Continual Data Streams. ACM SIGMOD, 13–24 (2001)
18. Gray, J., Chaudhuri, S., Bosworth, A., Layman, A., Reichart, D., Venkatrao, M.: Data Cube: A Relational Aggregation Operator Generalizing Group-By, Cross-Tab, and Sub-Totals. Data Mining and Knowledge Discovery 1(1), 29–53 (1997)
19. Han, J., Chen, Y., Dong, G., Pei, J., Wah, B., Wang, J., Cai, Y.: Stream Cube: An Architecture for Multi-Dimensional Analysis of Data Streams. Distributed and Parallel Databases 18(2), 173–197 (2005)
20. Ho, C.-T., Agrawal, R., Megiddo, N., Srikant, R.: Range Queries in OLAP Data Cubes. ACM SIGMOD, 73–88 (1997)
21. Iqbal, S., Bunn, J.J., Newman, H.B.: Distributed Heterogeneous Relational Data Warehouse in a Grid Environment. CHEP (2003), http://www.slac.stanford.edu/econf/C0303241/proc/papers/THAT007.pdf
22. Lawrence, M., Rau-Chaplin, A.: The OLAP-Enabled Grid: Model and Query Processing Algorithms. IEEE HPCS, 4–10 (2006)
23. Lawrence, M., Dehne, F.A., Rau-Chaplin, A.: Implementing OLAP Query Fragment Aggregation and Recombination for the OLAP Enabled Grid. IEEE IPDPS, 1–8 (2007)
24. Nguyen, M., Tjoa, A., Weippl, E., Brezany, P.: Toward a Grid-Based Zero-Latency Data Warehousing Implementation for Continuous Data Streams Processing. International Journal of Data Warehousing and Mining 1(4), 22–55 (2005)

25. Nieto-Santisteban, M.A., Gray, J., Szalay, A., Annis, J., Thakar, A.R., O'Mullane, W.: When Database Systems Meet the Grid. ACM CIDR, 154–161 (2005)
26. Muthukrishnan, S.: Data Streams: Algorithms and Applications. ACM-SIAM SODA, 413 (2003)
27. Poess, M., Othayoth, R.: Large Scale Data Warehouses on Grid: Oracle Database 10g and HP ProLiant Systems. In: VLDB, pp. 1055–1066 (2005)
28. Smith, J., Gounaris, A., Watson, P., Paton, N.W., Fernandes, A.A.A., Sakellariou, R.: Distributed Query Processing on the Grid. IEEE GRID, 279–290 (2002)
29. Stahl, F., Berrar, D.P., Silva, C., Rodrigues, R.J., Brito, R.M.M., Dubitzky, W.: Grid Warehousing of Molecular Dynamics Protein Unfolding Data. IEEE CCGRID, 496–503 (2005)
30. Wehrle, P., Miquel, M., Tchounikine, A.: A Model for Distributing and Querying a Data Warehouse on a Computing Grid. IEEE ICPADS, 203–209 (2005)
31. Wehrle, P., Miquel, M., Tchounikine, A.: A Grid Services-Oriented Architecture for Efficient Operation of Distributed Data Warehouses on Globus. IEEE AINA, 994–999 (2007)

Author Index

Lecture Notes in Computer Science

Sublibrary 3: Information Systems and Application, incl. Internet/Web and HCI

For information about Vols. 1– 4740
please contact your bookseller or Springer

Vol. 4936: W. Aiello, A. Broder, J. Janssen, E.E. Milios (Eds.), Algorithms and Models for the Web-Graph. X, 167 pages. 2008.

Vol. 4932: S. Hartmann, G. Kern-Isberner (Eds.), Foundations of Information and Knowledge Systems. XII, 397 pages. 2008.

Vol. 4928: A.H.M. ter Hofstede, B. Benatallah, H.-Y. Paik (Eds.), Business Process Management Workshops. XIII, 518 pages. 2008.

Vol. 4918: N. Boujemaa, M. Detyniecki, A. Nürnberger (Eds.), Adaptive Multimedial Retrieval: Retrieval, User, and Semantics. XI, 265 pages. 2008.

Vol. 4903: S. Satoh, F. Nack, M. Etoh (Eds.), Advances in Multimedia Modeling. XIX, 510 pages. 2008.

Vol. 4900: S. Spaccapietra (Ed.), Journal on Data Semantics X. XIII, 265 pages. 2008.

Vol. 4892: A. Popescu-Belis, S. Renals, H. Bourlard (Eds.), Machine Learning for Multimodal Interaction. XI, 308 pages. 2008.

Vol. 4882: T. Janowski, H. Mohanty (Eds.), Distributed Computing and Internet Technology. XIII, 346 pages. 2007.

Vol. 4881: H. Yin, P. Tino, E. Corchado, W. Byrne, X. Yao (Eds.), Intelligent Data Engineering and Automated Learning - IDEAL 2007. XX, 1174 pages. 2007.

Vol. 4877: C. Thanos, F. Borri, L. Candela (Eds.), Digital Libraries: Research and Development. XII, 350 pages. 2007.

Vol. 4872: D. Mery, L. Rueda (Eds.), Advances in Image and Video Technology. XXI, 961 pages. 2007.

Vol. 4871: M. Cavazza, S. Donikian (Eds.), Virtual Storytelling. XIII, 219 pages. 2007.

Vol. 4858: X. Deng, F.C. Graham (Eds.), Internet and Network Economics. XVI, 598 pages. 2007.

Vol. 4857: J.M. Ware, G.E. Taylor (Eds.), Web and Wireless Geographical Information Systems. XI, 293 pages. 2007.

Vol. 4853: F. Fonseca, M.A. Rodríguez, S. Levashkin (Eds.), GeoSpatial Semantics. X, 289 pages. 2007.

Vol. 4836: H. Ichikawa, W.-D. Cho, I. Satoh, H.Y. Youn (Eds.), Ubiquitous Computing Systems. XIII, 307 pages. 2007.

Vol. 4832: M. Weske, M.-S. Hacid, C. Godart (Eds.), Web Information Systems Engineering – WISE 2007 Workshops. XV, 518 pages. 2007.

Vol. 4831: B. Benatallah, F. Casati, D. Georgakopoulos, C. Bartolini, W. Sadiq, C. Godart (Eds.), Web Information Systems Engineering – WISE 2007. XVI, 675 pages. 2007.

Vol. 4825: K. Aberer, K.-S. Choi, N. Noy, D. Allemang, K.-I. Lee, L. Nixon, J. Golbeck, P. Mika, D. Maynard, R. Mizoguchi, G. Schreiber, P. Cudré-Mauroux (Eds.), The Semantic Web. XXVII, 973 pages. 2007.

Vol. 4823: H. Leung, F. Li, R. Lau, Q. Li (Eds.), Advances in Web Based Learning – ICWL 2007. XIV, 654 pages. 2008.

Vol. 4822: D.H.-L. Goh, T.H. Cao, I.T. Sølvberg, E. Rasmussen (Eds.), Asian Digital Libraries. XVII, 519 pages. 2007.

Vol. 4820: T.G. Wyeld, S. Kenderdine, M. Docherty (Eds.), Virtual Systems and Multimedia. XII, 215 pages. 2008.

Vol. 4816: B. Falcidieno, M. Spagnuolo, Y. Avrithis, I. Kompatsiaris, P. Buitelaar (Eds.), Semantic Multimedia. XII, 306 pages. 2007.

Vol. 4813: I. Oakley, S.A. Brewster (Eds.), Haptic and Audio Interaction Design. XIV, 145 pages. 2007.

Vol. 4810: H.H.-S. Ip, O.C. Au, H. Leung, M.-T. Sun, W.-Y. Ma, S.-M. Hu (Eds.), Advances in Multimedia Information Processing – PCM 2007. XXI, 834 pages. 2007.

Vol. 4809: M.K. Denko, C.-s. Shih, K.-C. Li, S.-L. Tsao, Q.-A. Zeng, S.H. Park, Y.-B. Ko, S.-H. Hung, J.-H. Park (Eds.), Emerging Directions in Embedded and Ubiquitous Computing. XXXV, 823 pages. 2007.

Vol. 4808: T.-W. Kuo, E. Sha, M. Guo, L.T. Yang, Z. Shao (Eds.), Embedded and Ubiquitous Computing. XXI, 769 pages. 2007.

Vol. 4806: R. Meersman, Z. Tari, P. Herrero (Eds.), On the Move to Meaningful Internet Systems 2007: OTM 2007 Workshops, Part II. XXXIV, 611 pages. 2007.

Vol. 4805: R. Meersman, Z. Tari, P. Herrero (Eds.), On the Move to Meaningful Internet Systems 2007: OTM 2007 Workshops, Part I. XXXIV, 757 pages. 2007.

Vol. 4804: R. Meersman, Z. Tari (Eds.), On the Move to Meaningful Internet Systems 2007: CoopIS, DOA, ODBASE, GADA, and IS, Part II. XXIX, 683 pages. 2007.

Vol. 4803: R. Meersman, Z. Tari (Eds.), On the Move to Meaningful Internet Systems 2007: CoopIS, DOA, ODBASE, GADA, and IS, Part I. XXIX, 1173 pages. 2007.

Vol. 4802: J.-L. Hainaut, E.A. Rundensteiner, M. Kirchberg, M. Bertolotto, M. Brochhausen, Y.-P.P. Chen, S.S.-S. Cherfi, M. Doerr, H. Han, S. Hartmann, J. Parsons, G. Poels, C. Rolland, J. Trujillo, E. Yu, E. Zimányie (Eds.), Advances in Conceptual Modeling – Foundations and Applications. XIX, 420 pages. 2007.

Vol. 4801: C. Parent, K.-D. Schewe, V.C. Storey, B. Thalheim (Eds.), Conceptual Modeling - ER 2007. XVI, 616 pages. 2007.

Vol. 4797: M. Arenas, M.I. Schwartzbach (Eds.), Database Programming Languages. VIII, 261 pages. 2007.

Vol. 4796: M. Lew, N. Sebe, T.S. Huang, E.M. Bakker (Eds.), Human–Computer Interaction. X, 157 pages. 2007.

Vol. 4794: B. Schiele, A.K. Dey, H. Gellersen, B. de Ruyter, M. Tscheligi, R. Wichert, E. Aarts, A. Buchmann (Eds.), Ambient Intelligence. XV, 375 pages. 2007.

Vol. 4777: S. Bhalla (Ed.), Databases in Networked Information Systems. X, 329 pages. 2007.

Vol. 4761: R. Obermaisser, Y. Nah, P. Puschner, F.J. Rammig (Eds.), Software Technologies for Embedded and Ubiquitous Systems. XIV, 563 pages. 2007.

Vol. 4747: S. Džeroski, J. Struyf (Eds.), Knowledge Discovery in Inductive Databases. X, 301 pages. 2007.

Vol. 4744: Y. de Kort, W. IJsselsteijn, C. Midden, B. Eggen, B.J. Fogg (Eds.), Persuasive Technology. XIV, 316 pages. 2007.